D0814598

101

Ways to Score Higher on Your

MCAT®:

What You Need to Know About the Medical College Admission Test® Explained Simply

By Marti Anne Maguire
With Paula Stiles

CHICAGO HEIGHTS PUBLIC LIBRARY

610.76
M21
c.1

101 WAYS TO SCORE HIGHER ON YOUR MCAT: WHAT YOU NEED TO KNOW ABOUT THE MEDICAL COLLEGE ADMISSION TEST EXPLAINED SIMPLY

Copyright © 2010 Atlantic Publishing Group, Inc.
1405 SW 6th Avenue • Ocala, Florida 34471 • Phone 800-814-1132 • Fax 352-622-1875
Web site: www.atlantic-pub.com • E-mail: sales@atlantic-pub.com
SAN Number: 268-1250

No part of this publication may be reproduced, stored in a retrieval system, or transmitted in any form or by any means, electronic, mechanical, photocopying, recording, scanning, or otherwise, except as permitted under Section 107 or 108 of the 1976 United States Copyright Act, without the prior written permission of the Publisher. Requests to the Publisher for permission should be sent to Atlantic Publishing Group, Inc., 1405 SW 6th Avenue, Ocala, Florida 34471.

Library of Congress Cataloging-in-Publication Data

Maguire, Marti Anne.
  101 ways to score higher on your MCAT : what you need to know about the medical college admission test explained simply / by Marti Maguire.
     p. cm.
  Includes bibliographical references and index.
  ISBN-13: 978-1-60138-251-1 (alk. paper)
  ISBN-10: 1-60138-251-0 (alk. paper)
  1. Medical College Admission Test--Study guides. I. Title. II. Title: One hundred one ways to score higher on your MCAT. III. Title: One hundred and one ways to score higher on your MCAT.
  R838.5.M25 2010
  610.76--dc22
                                2010009564

All trademarks, trade names, or logos mentioned or used are the property of their respective owners and are used only to directly describe the products being provided. Every effort has been made to properly capitalize, punctuate, identify and attribute trademarks and trade names to their respective owners, including the use of ® and ™ wherever possible and practical. Atlantic Publishing Group, Inc. is not a partner, affiliate, or licensee with the holders of said trademarks.

MCAT® and Medical College Admission Test® is a registered service mark of the Association of American Medical Colleges, which does not endorse this study guide or methodology.

LIMIT OF LIABILITY/DISCLAIMER OF WARRANTY: The publisher and the author make no representations or warranties with respect to the accuracy or completeness of the contents of this work and specifically disclaim all warranties, including without limitation warranties of fitness for a particular purpose. No warranty may be created or extended by sales or promotional materials. The advice and strategies contained herein may not be suitable for every situation. This work is sold with the understanding that the publisher is not engaged in rendering legal, accounting, or other professional services. If professional assistance is required, the services of a competent professional should be sought. Neither the publisher nor the author shall be liable for damages arising herefrom. The fact that an organization or Web site is referred to in this work as a citation and/or a potential source of further information does not mean that the author or the publisher endorses the information the organization or Web site may provide or recommendations it may make. Further, readers should be aware that Internet Web sites listed in this work may have changed or disappeared between when this work was written and when it is read.

Printed in the United States

PROJECT MANAGER: Erin Everhart • eeverhart@atlantic-pub.com
PEER REVIEWER: Marilee Griffin • mgriffin@atlantic-pub.com
ASSISTANT EDITOR: Angela Pham • apham@atlantic-pub.com
EDITORIAL INTERN: Nedda Pourahmady • npourahmady@atlantic-pub.com
PRE PRESS & PRODUCTION DESIGN: Holly Marie Gibbs • hgibbs@atlantic-pub.com
INTERIOR DESIGN: Samantha Martin • smartin@atlantic-pub.com
FRONT & BACK COVER DESIGN: Jackie Miller • millerjackiej@gmail.com

Printed on Recycled Paper

We recently lost our beloved pet "Bear," who was not only our best and dearest friend but also the "Vice President of Sunshine" here at Atlantic Publishing. He did not receive a salary but worked tirelessly 24 hours a day to please his parents. Bear was a rescue dog that turned around and showered myself, my wife, Sherri, his grandparents Jean, Bob, and Nancy, and every person and animal he met (maybe not rabbits) with friendship and love. He made a lot of people smile every day.

We wanted you to know that a portion of the profits of this book will be donated to The Humane Society of the United States. *–Douglas & Sherri Brown*

The human-animal bond is as old as human history. We cherish our animal companions for their unconditional affection and acceptance. We feel a thrill when we glimpse wild creatures in their natural habitat or in our own backyard.

Unfortunately, the human-animal bond has at times been weakened. Humans have exploited some animal species to the point of extinction.

The Humane Society of the United States makes a difference in the lives of animals here at home and worldwide. The HSUS is dedicated to creating a world where our relationship with animals is guided by compassion. We seek a truly humane society in which animals are respected for their intrinsic value, and where the human-animal bond is strong.

Want to help animals? We have plenty of suggestions. Adopt a pet from a local shelter, join The Humane Society and be a part of our work to help companion animals and wildlife. You will be funding our educational, legislative, investigative and outreach projects in the U.S. and across the globe.

Or perhaps you'd like to make a memorial donation in honor of a pet, friend or relative? You can through our Kindred Spirits program. And if you'd like to contribute in a more structured way, our Planned Giving Office has suggestions about estate planning, annuities, and even gifts of stock that avoid capital gains taxes.

Maybe you have land that you would like to preserve as a lasting habitat for wildlife. Our Wildlife Land Trust can help you. Perhaps the land you want to share is a backyard—that's enough. Our Urban Wildlife Sanctuary Program will show you how to create a habitat for your wild neighbors.

So you see, it's easy to help animals. And The HSUS is here to help.

THE HUMANE SOCIETY
OF THE UNITED STATES.

2100 L Street NW • Washington, DC 20037 • 202-452-1100
www.hsus.org

dedication

To the Concerned Reader, who is my most loyal fan.

toc

table of contents

Part Two

introduction

Every year, thousands of premed students take the Medical College Admissions Test®, or MCAT®, in hopes of gaining entry into medical school. In turn, the white-robed dreams of many capable would-be doctors have perished in the wake of this daunting test, which requires you not only to know all of the major concepts of physics, chemistry, and biology, but to also be able to combine and apply them to completely unfamiliar situations. The test also includes sections on writing and reading comprehension — not exactly the cup of tea for most prospective doctors.

So, yes, others have failed, but your fate could be different. As is the case for higher education of nearly any sort today — the SAT for undergraduate education, the LSAT for law school, and so on — the MCAT is a hurdle that simply must be cleared before you can be a doctor. Period. This book will give you the skills to run faster and jump higher so you can clear this hurdle that lies in your path to medical school, provided you are prepared to train and practice like an Olympic contender.

As the standard entrance exam in the United States and Canada, the MCAT has a formidable reputation as a tough exam, and it seems to only get tougher. Some test watchers claim that the Association of American Medical Colleges (AAMC), which administers the test, has made the test progressively more difficult over the years so that it would continue to help medical schools winnow out applicants even as the number of applications they saw rose. Still, there is a silver lining on the MCAT cloud. If you have taken the basic undergraduate premed prerequisites, you should be familiar with every concept that will show up on the MCAT.

101 Ways to Score Higher on Your MCAT is intended to supplement, not replace, your premed courses. It will help you improve your score on the MCAT, but it should not be used as your sole method of study. This type of study aid can be useful, whether you are having difficulties with MCAT material or just want a quick review of what will be on the test before you take it. You can improve your score by learning the subjects, as well as the nature of the test itself. This does not mean cheating or finding out answers beforehand, but instead familiarizing yourself with the overall format of the test and the broad array of knowledge that will be expected from you.

Familiarizing yourself with the MCAT will also help you reduce your anxiety before and during the test. Test anxiety is one of the greatest barriers to a high score for otherwise excellent students. By getting to know the structure, nature, and contents of the MCAT, you can reduce your test anxiety considerably. There is no need to approach MCAT as an unknown entity.

This book is organized into two parts. Part I discusses the logistics of applying for and taking the test. It also discusses how to prepare for the test, including test-taking tips and strategies. Part II offers a review of the material you will find on the test, with sample questions and other study materials to help you practice. The chapters in Part II correspond to the format that you will use on the test. It is best for you to study the subjects in the same order you will encounter them on the test. This will help you organize your knowledge of the subjects in a way that facilitates your comprehension. This book will also help you with basic, college-level algebra and trigonometry exercises, as you will need these skills to answer the questions, particularly in the physics and general chemistry sections, but also the verbal reasoning section.

The writing sample chapter differs from the other chapters in the book, which also reflects the difference between the writing portion and the other parts of the test. The chapters for the other sections have multiple-choice question sets and are graded numerically, as you will find in the test. The two essays in the writing sample section in the test are graded holistically. Therefore, the writing sample chapter will consist of a quick tutorial on how to write the kind of essay that the MCAT will expect from you. It will also include practice essays written from prompts to give you an idea of what quality level of essay gets you what grade.

So do not edge that white coat out of your dreams just yet. If you are willing to buckle down for some serious training, you will find your way past the MCAT hurdle and on to medical school with this book.

PART

01

chapter

01

MCAT Basics

Before we can get into the nitty-gritty of MCAT content, you will probably want to know about the nuts and bolts of taking the test, from why you have to take it to when you will get your scores. Here are answers to some of the most common questions about the test.

Mastering the MCAT

The information below should cover most general questions about the MCAT. If the answer to your question is not listed here, use the list of resources in the back of the book to find more information to answer your specific questions.

General Information

What is the MCAT?

The MCAT is an admissions test written and administered by the Association of American Medical Colleges (AAMC). It was first instituted in 1991 and is now used as a nearly universal tool in North America for entry into medical school. Since 2007, it has been offered only as a computer-based test (CBT). The actual test lasts for four hours and 20 minutes. With breaks and other delays, the overall testing period will exceed five hours.

Who must take the MCAT?

Any student who wishes to enter medical school, including veterinary schools, in the United States or Canada must take the MCAT — and to get into most schools, those students must score well. MCAT is used as a major tool by those institutions in determining what students to accept. Other factors, such as grades and personal statements, are also important criteria, but if you do poorly on the MCAT, you are not likely to get into medical school.

Why must you take the MCAT?

The MCAT is an important diagnostic tool used by medical schools to evaluate, rank, and choose what applicants they will take. It is, however, just *one* of the tools that admission personnel use to evaluate the applicant's strengths and weaknesses, along with his or her grades, experience, and the other elements of the application. The MCAT also measures the applicant's overall aptitude in the fields that are required for the medical profession. The MCAT is not the only criterion used by medical schools for entry, but it is a major one, so you will need to do well on it.

Where can you take the MCAT?

The MCAT can be taken at any officially sanctioned Thomson-Prometric testing center (the company that administers the MCAT for the AAMC), usually at your local college or university. Check the AAMC Web site (**www.aamc.org/mcat**) for local test centers in your area.

When is the MCAT administered?

The MCAT is administered on at least 26 test dates, held each year between January and September. You can choose to take the MCAT in the morning, afternoon, or on weekends, depending on your schedule and the availability of the nearest test center. See the official Web site for the current schedule, registration deadlines, and test times. Generally, you must sign up for the test two weeks in advance.

Mastering the MCAT

Do not plan to take the MCAT in September if you are applying to begin school the next year. In the rare event that a test is canceled for one of these test dates, you will not have another chance to take the test until January. That means you will miss the application deadline for most medical schools, which are generally between October and December. Ideally, you want to take the test earlier, anyway, so that you have time to take it again if needed.

How much does the MCAT cost?

The registration fee for the MCAT is $230. You will be charged an extra $55 for late registration (up to a week before the test), to change your test date, or to change the location of your test. You will pay an extra $65 to take the test outside of the United States, U.S. territories, or Canada. The MCAT offers a fee assistance program for prospective test takers whose income falls below certain federal guidelines. For 2010, an applicant whose family income was less than 300 percent of the poverty level, based on family size, was eligible for fee assistance. For instance, for 2009–2010, a member of a family of four with a household income of less than $66,150 a year would be eligible for assistance. Applicants must be approved for fee assistance before they register for the MCAT. Register at **www.aamc.org/ students/applying/fap**.

When should you take the MCAT?

Ideally, you should take the MCAT about a year before your application for medical school is due. This will ensure that you have your results ready when you apply, and you will also have time to re-take it if you are not happy with your scores.

Mastering the MCAT

Do not take the MCAT any earlier than three years prior to when you will apply to medical school because some medical schools will not accept MCAT scores older than three years. Others will accept them for five years.

What is the electronic MCAT?

Currently, the MCAT is administered solely as a computer-based test, in which you see questions and submit answers to them on a computer screen. The essays, likewise, are typed into a word processing program. Before 2007, the MCAT was administered as a longer, paper-and-pencil test only twice a year. Beyond the more frequent test dates, the computer format is also shorter and allows scores to be reported about twice as quickly as they were for the paper-and-pencil test. Taking the computer test does not require any particular skills, but you will likely benefit from some practice with it before test day.

How is the MCAT scored?

Your overall MCAT score consists of four separate scores corresponding to the four separate sections of the test. Your score will also be calculated as a combined score ranging from 3 to 45 for all three multiple-choice sections of the test. The multiple-choice sections are each scored on a scale of 1 (lowest) to 15 (highest), with 8 being the average, and 10 or higher being above average.

The writing section is scored separately from the multiple-choice sections. The two essays are lumped together and given a letter score from J (lowest) to T (highest) based on scores of one to six given by two graders. A test taker with an O has an average mark, but more test takers get either an M (low average) or a Q (high average) than any other mark. In general, the writing section is not considered as heavily in admissions decisions as the other sections of the test — unless your writing score happens to be particularly good, which will help you, or particularly bad, which will hurt you. In addition, most medical schools would prefer to see scores that are balanced between sections. For instance, scores of 8, 10, and 12 on the three sections would be preferable to scores of 5, 6, and 19, even though both sets of scores add up to 30.

The following are the average MCAT scores among applicants accepted to medical schools for the 2008–2009 school year. The numbers denote the average from 1–15 between the three multiple-choice sections, along with the writing score.

Stanford University	11.7Q
Yale University	11.7Q
University of Florida	10.7P
Louisiana State University	9.3P
Harvard University	11.7R
Texas A&M	9.7O

University of North Carolina at Chapel Hill	IIQ

When will you get your scores, and how do you send them to medical schools?

A score report will arrive in the mail about four weeks after you take the test, or you can access your scores online from the AAMC MCAT site 30 days after you take the test. Your scores are available through a centrally run system known as MCAT Testing History System, or THx, which allows you to select schools to view your scores once you have released them. If you are applying to a school that participates in the American Medical College Application Service (as most do), they will be able to access the scores through THx. You will not have to pay to send your scores to schools. For schools that do not participate in this program, you can print out a copy of your scores for free and send them through the mail.

Can you take the test more than once?

You are free to take the MCAT more than once if you feel your score does not reflect your abilities, though you should know that the score reports you send to schools would include your scores from every time you took the test. So even if your later scores are better, those schools may consider your earlier, lower scores in their admissions decisions. For that reason, it is better to sufficiently study before you take the test the first time. You are allowed to take the MCAT as many as three times in one calendar year, but you cannot register for more than one test at a time.

Mastering the MCAT

It is generally not worthwhile to take the test more than once unless you plan to study intensely or take a course in a subject that is covered on the test between test administrations — unless there was some particular reason for your low score, such as misunderstanding instructions.

What scores do schools use if you take the test twice?

Different colleges and universities have their own policies for how to deal with scores. According to surveys of schools conducted by the AAMC, most consider your scores from each test you took equally, noting improvements between test administrations. Other schools look at the most recent scores or an average of all of your scores. Some schools will consider a composite score created by using your highest score on each section of the test. You may inquire to individual schools about their policies.

How heavily is the MCAT weighed in medical school admissions?

As with most standardized admissions tests, the way the MCAT is weighed will vary significantly from one medical school to another. However, most consider your MCAT score as only one part of your overall application, along with your college grades, letters of recommendation, and experience. Some schools will have a minimum score in mind, while some will admit applicants with less-stellar scores if other parts of the application warrant such an exception. The test may also be used to assess your strengths and weaknesses in particular academic areas, and admissions officers will likely make note if your MCAT scores do not mesh with your grades in the appropriate courses.

What are the policies concerning cheating?

The MCAT test centers have a very strict policy against cheating and take steps to ensure that none will occur. You will not be allowed to bring any materials into the testing area, including books, study materials (such as formula sheets), and calculators. You will receive scratch paper and a pencil to write out any notes for problem solving. If you need to write out an equation for a question or do any arithmetic, you can use the scratch paper.

Mastering the MCAT

Any activity that might appear to be cheating, including any form of communication between students, is strictly forbidden and can result in being banned from the testing area without a refund. Needless to say, such a mark on your record will not encourage medical schools to take you, even if you attend the MCAT later on and legitimately do well. Observe these restrictions closely, come prepared, and come without aids.

Is the MCAT available in multiple languages?

No: The test is only administered in English. This is because both correspondence with the AAMC and instruction in medical schools in the United States and Canada are in English. You will be required to have sufficient English proficiency in reading and writing English to understand and answer the questions, as well as to write the two essays. If this is a problem for you because English is your second language, you should consider taking additional English instruction before sitting for the MCAT.

Will the MCAT accommodate disabilities or other issues?

Known as "accommodated testing," MCAT testing conditions can be modified for those with a disability or other problems that make it difficult for them to take the test. These can include both chronic and temporary physical and psychological disabilities that would require some change in the testing environment in order for someone to be able to take the test under reasonable and comfortable conditions. The AAMC will make changes to the MCAT for those with conditions such as diabetes, learning disabilities, and a variety of physical impairments. The accommodations made include presenting the test in large print, allowing test takers to take the test in a separate room, bring in an inhaler or water, or even take extra time to complete the test. The AAMC evaluates applications on a case-by-case basis, so if you have a need for accommodation, you should contact the Office of Accommodated Testing at least 60 days before your test to ensure your request is processed in time. *See the back of this book for contact information.*

chapter

Inside the MCAT

The MCAT can be a difficult test, but it is not insurmountable. The individual questions are meant to be tricky more than downright difficult, and while there are many of them, there are not so many that you cannot get through them in the allotted time. If all else fails, just remember that you are not the only one who will find the MCAT difficult. Everyone else taking it with you is probably just as nervous. There is no perfect MCAT test taker you will be compared against. Using this book is an excellent first step in your preparation for the test. Beyond that, you will need to know precisely what you will be facing when you sit down to take the MCAT, both in terms of content and the format of the test.

Mastering the MCAT

Unlike some standardized tests (such as the SAT Reasoning Test), the MCAT has no penalties for wrong answers. You should therefore answer all questions to ensure that you receive the highest score possible. Guessing when you have no other way of determining the answer will not hurt you on the MCAT as it would on the SAT.

The Format

To start, you should know that the test is divided into the following four sections:

1. Physical sciences (including both physics and general chemistry)
2. Verbal reasoning
3. Writing sample
4. Biological sciences (including both biology and organic chemistry)

All of the sections are multiple-choice, except for the writing sample, in which you will write two essays. All four sections involve information that can be found in first-year college courses, though the approach of the questions will often be quite different from what you might have seen in your college classes; that is because the test is designed to measure how well you reason through unfamiliar issues. The writing prompts are generally not scientific and may deal with ethics, the social sciences, or other topics that are accessible to a wide audience.

In addition to the four sections, you will also have various breaks and help periods. The test begins with an optional five-minute tutorial on the mechanics of taking the computer-based test. After that, you are given an optional 10-minute break after each section. The test ends with an optional 10-minute survey and some time to allow you to void your scores if you feel you did poorly. *This option is discussed further in the "During the Test" section in Chapter 5.*

Mastering the MCAT

Though the periodic breaks and the initial tutorial are optional, it is highly recommended that you take advantage of them. The MCAT is a long and grueling exam. Do not overexert yourself by ignoring the breaks scheduled for you; they are there to make sure you do not let fatigue affect your score.

The MCAT also differs from other computerized tests, such as the Graduate Record Examination, or GRE, in that it is not adaptive. When you take the GRE you receive certain questions based on how you answered previous questions. For instance, if you answer a question correctly, you will be given a more difficult question than if you had answered the question incorrectly. Tests that follow this system are known as "adaptive tests," because the tests adapt to the responses of the person taking it. The MCAT is not an adaptive test, so you will receive the same test regardless of your answers.

The computer-based test

The MCAT is now only available in the computer-based version, which is intended to be a simpler way to take the test. It should be just that if you are used to using a computer, whether a PC or a Mac. However, the format does have its own quirks that you must get used to, and it might help you to practice in advance, particularly if you do not adapt well to new computer programs.

Mastering the MCAT

Because the computer-based test has its own learning curve, the tutorial may not be enough time for you to learn it properly. Therefore, it is wise to familiarize yourself with the mouse and keyboard commands that you will need to know before you take the test.

First, you can access the periodic table of the elements by pressing a specially marked button on your computer keyboard. You can also highlight text in a passage that you think might be important later on by clicking on it (clicking again will remove the highlight). On the test, however, this highlighting will only remain until you move on to the next passage. You can also use the "strikeout" capability, which allows you to eliminate wrong answers as you proceed through a question by left clicking on them with the mouse. The strikeouts will remain even after you have moved onto another passage.

There are several other keyboard commands to be aware of when taking the test. Along the bottom of the screen are a timer and several buttons. The "previous" and "next" buttons allow you to go to the next and previous pages of the test. A "review" button allows you to go to a summary of the section on which you are working. From that screen, you can click on any question number to go to that question. A "mark" option at the bottom of your screen will allow you to flag a question within a section if you want to come back to it later, should you reach the end and have time to go back.

There are several significant differences between the official MCAT and the online practice tests that are available from AAMC and other sources. Several key commands found on the practice tests do not exist on the official test, namely the search, notes, and guess functions. The search function helps you find a word or phrase in a passage. The notes function allows you to insert electronic notes into the test as you go along. The guess box gives you hints when you are having difficulty with the question.

Mastering the MCAT

Know which keyboard commands you can use on the practice tests but that do not exist on the actual test. The electronic notes you can make during the practice tests, for example, are not an option on the actual test. You will only receive scratch paper and a pencil on which to write down formulas and solve equations. To better prepare for the test, do not use these commands when you practice.

In the practice test, you can use the highlight function to highlight sections of a passage and move on to a passage without losing the highlighting, though this is not true with the official MCAT. Likewise, in the practice test, the questions that you eliminate using the strikeout key are cleared after you leave the section, but in the official MCAT, those strikeouts stay even after you move on to the next section.

Content

Within each section are a myriad of concepts that you should be sure you know before you take the test. A full chapter of this book will be devoted to the concepts included in each of the test's first four sections. For now, however, we offer a brief rundown of MCAT content.

Physical sciences

The physical sciences section will be the first section of the MCAT. It lasts 70 minutes and consists of 52 questions about physics and general physical chemistry. These come in clusters of five to seven questions derived from seven or nine passages that lay out an experiment or scientific problem, followed by supplementary material such as graphs, tables, and formulas. Think of these clusters as solving the problem in multiple-choice form. The section also includes ten to 13 "freestanding" questions unrelated to the passages. The physical sciences section can include question clusters from:

Physics

☑	Force
☑	Momentum
☑	Friction
☑	Vectors
☑	Equilibrium

✓	Systems
✓	Torque
✓	Waves
✓	Light
✓	Optics

Physical chemistry

✓	States and phases (solids, liquids, and gasses)
✓	Stoichiometry
✓	Thermodynamics
✓	Acids and bases
✓	Electrochemistry

Some questions might cross over between physics and chemistry, such as those involving equilibrium and phase changes.

Verbal reasoning

The verbal reasoning section is the second part of the test. Similar to the reading comprehension part of the SAT Reasoning Test, it lasts for 60 minutes and consists of 40 questions about reading comprehension based on seven passages averaging 699 words. These passages can be taken from either books or articles from a wide variety of disciplines both in the sciences and the humanities. Most of these questions will focus on the main idea of the passage, and the author's approach and main arguments. Few will concentrate on the actual facts in the articles. The verbal reasoning section might include:

Verbal Reasoning

✓	History
✓	Science
✓	Political science
✓	Art
✓	Literature

You will need to determine and understand the main idea for most of the passages, but questions might also involve the author's tone or approach, the context of certain sentences, and vocabulary.

Writing sample

This section lasts for 60 minutes, in which you will write two essays in response to the given prompts, which are statements or questions presenting the subject of the essay. Usually the prompt will consist of a general statement and three writing tasks for you to perform. Your essays will need to answer these prompts using clearly defined arguments.

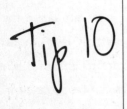

Mastering the MCAT

While the graders will take into consideration that you are writing an essay under a strict time limit, you should still attempt to demonstrate your knowledge of basic writing skills as much as possible. The essays are graded both on the strength of your arguments and the clarity of your writing, which includes making appropriate word choices and adhering to grammatical rules.

That said, the essay graders are most interested in how well you address the assignment and how clearly you communicate. You do not need to be Shakespeare or Hemingway to do well on the writing sample section.

Biological sciences

The last section of the MCAT, biological sciences, lasts for 70 minutes and consists of 52 questions. The biological sciences section has the same format as that of the physical sciences section, and only the subject matter of the questions differs. The biological sciences section can include question clusters from:

Biology

✓	Human biology
✓	Pathogens and immunity
✓	Molecular biology
✓	Structures of the cell

Organic Chemistry

✓	Molecular chemistry
✓	Functional groups
✓	Reactions and products
✓	Macromolecules
✓	Lab techniques

chapter 03

Studying for the MCAT

That long list of concepts you just read might prompt some (understandable) questions. Where do I start? How will I ever learn all of this? Should I just give up now? However, there is no reason to despair. Now that you know what lies ahead for you on the MCAT, you can devise a study plan that will allow you to maximize your score. In this chapter, you will learn how to develop a study plan, and you will also see a wealth of tips for studying effectively.

Study and test-taking strategies can mean the difference between a good test and a great test — even a good testing experience and a bad testing experience. Take the time to schedule your study as well as the time to organize yourself *before* the test. If you plan your study, this will maximize what you get out of it. If you go into the MCAT already organized in your thinking and aware of the test structure, this will help you relax and maximize your performance. Doing these things may take a little extra time, but it is worth it.

Practice Tests

Mastering the MCAT

As you complete practice tests, be sure to do as many computer-based tests as possible. The computer is not hard to use. However, as you do practice tests, you build up small habits, from how you highlight important parts of passages to how you eliminate wrong answer choices, which makes the test feel natural to you. That higher comfort level can translate to a higher score. Try to build those habits on the computer instead of through pencil and paper.

A big part of your study plan should be taking MCAT practice tests. Completing practice tests starting at least six months before you take the actual test will help you figure out where your weak areas are, so you will know where to focus your study time. Practice tests will also get you accustomed to the format of the questions and the way the computer test works. Remember: Half the battle is knowing how to take the test.

The AAMC provides practice MCAT tests on its site. However, all of them require registration, and only one test is free. Beyond that, you will pay $35 per test, a fee that will allow you to access that test for a one-year period. These are the gold-standard practice tests because they come straight from the source. However, you will find other free practice tests online that, in addition to the AAMC practice tests, will help you get used to the MCAT format and concepts. The Princeton Review, for instance, offers a free, full-length online practice test at its Web site, **www.princetonreview.com/ medical/free-mcat-practice-test.aspx**. Other online resources will offer targeted practice in the test's various subjects. For instance, at Test Prep Review (**www.testprepreview.com/mcat_practice.htm**), you will find self-assessment quizzes in nearly every topic found on the test.

Mastering the MCAT

You can buy books that will include several practice tests, though this is only really necessary if you exhaust the free tests found online or would prefer to use a single book to save the time you would spend searching.

Practice tests will help you learn some of the topics on the test, but more so it will help you learn the test itself. Studying the test will help you know what to expect, and that will help you reduce your anxiety. Becoming familiar with the structure of the test will also help you concentrate and prevent surprises.

Scheduling Study Time

Your two major enemies in the MCAT are time and anxiety. Many students score poorly on the MCAT because they did not organize themselves well beforehand, or they allowed their anxiety to interfere with their test performance. Therefore, taking the time to get organized before you begin studying is critical. Time management is a two-fold issue: You need to get organized so that you make the most of your studying leading up to the test, and you must practice managing your time during the test so you can get the most out of the limited time you have. Being fully prepared will also make you less anxious about taking the test.

Mastering the MCAT

Finding time to prepare for a test such as the MCAT is challenging. To start, your most important strategy will be to set aside time to study and stick to those times. Chart out specific periods of time when you will study, then avoid the temptation to make excuses when the time comes.

To accomplish both goals, you should start studying for the MCAT at least three months ahead of time, but preferably up to a year in advance if you feel you have a lot of material to cover before test day. While the material covered on the MCAT is based on first-year college courses, you may have some difficulty with the test if you have not quite mastered the material in standard premed courses such as calculus and organic chemistry — or if many years have passed since you took these courses. In any case, you will need to leave plenty of time to complete practice tests and exercises so you will be familiar with the test format and content. It can be difficult to complete the different tasks involved in studying and registering for the MCAT. Trying to do so also takes up mental capacity that you could be using in actual study.

Hang the calendar on your wall, within easy reach and view. This will help remind you to focus on that goal. When it is hanging on your wall in front of you, it is hard to forget about it or put it out of your mind, and therefore harder to procrastinate studying. Listing all of these tasks in one place helps you better organize your goals. You can mark each goal off as you complete it, and you will soon get a sense of how much studying you can realistically complete in your set time period. Seeing your progress can also help motivate you when you feel as though studying may never end.

Mastering the MCAT

To keep track of everything from registration deadlines to your study schedule, try keeping a separate calendar just for the MCAT. Depending on how long you have to study, a monthly calendar may be sufficient, or you may need a yearly calendar. Whatever you choose, you should get a format that encompasses as much of your study schedule as possible on one page.

Ideally, the MCAT would be the only test for which you would be studying. However, you might find yourself juggling the MCAT with premed or other college courses. When studying for the test, you might need to use time that you would normally devote to other courses. One way to cope with the lack of time is to pick periods when you will naturally have less homework, such as the beginning of the semester before major homework is assigned, and during holidays, such as winter break, spring break, and summer vacation. You might find you have to sacrifice some free time by doing this.

You will need a plan to make sure that you will have enough time to study everything. While you can memorize some information quickly, other skills such as essay writing, problem solving, and reading comprehension require long-term studying. Even memorization takes time, especially for physics formulas and organic chemistry equations, which can be quite complex and difficult to remember.

Steps to successful studying

Now that you have learned to set aside the time you will need to study, you must use that time as effectively as possible. If you follow these steps, you will avoid many of the study pitfalls that test takers often discover only after they take the test.

1. Set a goal

One of your first steps as you develop your study plan should be to set an overall goal for what you want to accomplish with your studies. Your goal could be a specific score or level of familiarity with each subject. Once you have your overall goal, you can set smaller goals for each week that you are studying.

Aim for the score you need to help you achieve your goal of going to medical school instead of a dream score. While what constitutes a "good score" will vary from school to school, a score of 30 is generally considered good enough to get you in the running for most programs. So, to be safe, try for a score of 32. Also, check into the average scores at the school you are looking for and set your goal accordingly. If you struggle on tests, have limited time to study, and know your application will have other outstanding features, cut yourself a break and set a slightly lower goal.

Mastering the MCAT

Set goals and stick to them. If you realize you cannot stick to them, revise them into goals that you can do. Be realistic but also disciplined. Do not set unrealistic goals. That will only discourage you, making it less likely you will achieve even a more modest level of success.

2. Gather your materials

You do not want to sit down for your first study session, only to find that you will need to spend that whole session — and then some — gathering the various things you will need to study. To maximize your study time, gather everything you will need before your first study session and keep it all in one centralized place, such as your desk or office.

Mastering the MCAT

Before you sit down to study, make sure that you have found (or purchased) practice tests, bought a calendar, and have access to a computer while you study; you will need it to complete practice tests, and likely for other research. You should also dig up your college textbooks from the courses. Make sure your study area is stocked with pencils, paper, highlighters, sticky notes, and whatever else you use when you study.

3. Study the test

Next, you will need to familiarize yourself with the test and the content it covers. To do this, complete at least one full-length practice test, then spend some time reviewing that test. Make notes of which questions were most difficult for you and what made them so challenging. Did you not know the content, or was it hard for you to apply your knowledge to the questions asked? Do you understand why you missed the questions you missed? Next, re-familiarize yourself with the relevant subjects by reviewing the later chapters of this book. Based on your memory of these subjects and your performance on the practice test, note which of the subjects listed here are most difficult for you:

☐	Physics
☐	Physical chemistry
☐	Organic chemistry
☐	Biology
☐	Algebra

☐	Trigonometry
☐	Reading comprehension
☐	Writing skill

Studying the test in this way accomplishes two things. First, it helps you narrow down your area of study to manageable levels. Not everything that you study in your college courses for these various disciplines will appear on the MCAT. You will find questions and situations related to the medical field, except in the reading comprehension and essay sections. These sections can focus on the physical sciences as well as social science, literature, and a host of other areas.

Mastering the MCAT

A major enemy in the MCAT is expecting more than the test will actually cover. The MCAT is already difficult enough. Do not make it seem even more intimidating by studying as if every scientific concept you have ever studied may show up on the test. This will only serve to waste your time and sap your self-confidence.

Second, studying how the test is set up helps you determine how to answer questions in the MCAT format. You will be studying subjects that you have studied for four to eight years in college and high school. The MCAT, however, is going to approach these topics in a different way, because the test is meant to assess not just how well you know these subjects, but how well you will be able to reason through new material. Familiarizing yourself with the way the MCAT asks questions will make it less of a shock when you are sitting in the testing center.

4. Create a study plan

Now that you know what the test looks like and where your weaknesses are, you can create a study plan that will help you maximize your score to the greatest extent possible in the amount of time you have to study. Try to establish how much you can reasonably study in a given day and schedule it ahead of time, knowing that you can tweak the plan if needed. Set goals for the next month. For example, a two-month review could go like this:

2-Month Review

Week 1	Review the test structure, complete first practice test
Week 2	Review the overall subjects
Week 3	Establish which subjects need extra study time and review them
Week 4	Start practice exercises in the physical sciences section
Week 5	Start practice exercises in verbal reasoning and mathematical techniques
Week 6	Start practice essays in the writing sample section
Week 7	Start practice exercises in the biological sciences section
Week 8	More practice tests

Mastering the MCAT

As you develop your study plan, use your time wisely by separating "study" from "practice." For example, memorize formulas and use them in practice exercises. There is a big difference between studying and doing practice questions, and your practice will be more effective if you have already studied the concepts you will be using.

For each week, schedule study times and log them onto your calendar in pencil, trying to choose times in the day that are best for your body clock. It is better to break down your studying into smaller tasks that are more manageable and less intimidating. For example, you can decide to memorize formulas in one study session, balance equations in another session, do practice questions in a third session, and do a practice test in a fourth. You may want to leave out a particularly difficult question set and work on it in a separate session, devoting extra time to it. Break your study of each section down to tasks as small and basic as they need to be for you to manage them.

Mastering the MCAT

When you study, start slow and build up. The MCAT can seem overwhelmingly large and complex, so break it down into manageable tasks. For example, instead of trying to study physics and physical chemistry at once, choose one and study it thoroughly, then move on to the next one.

As you plan your study schedule, try not to crowd too much material into too short of a time period. Even though the subjects on the MCAT are ones for which you have already studied and taken classes for, you still need to leave a sufficient amount of time to ensure full coverage without short-changing one of your subjects. That said, make sure that your study plan only includes topics that are part of the MCAT, not all of trigonometry, for instance. This book will help you narrow down your focus on what is actually on the test.

Mastering the MCAT

You want your plan to be thorough, but in the right way. Studying too broadly can get you into almost as much trouble as not studying enough. Keep in mind that the MCAT is not a general science test. Therefore, the science questions will all relate to the medical field. This will help you narrow your focus and avoid wasting time studying concepts that will not be on the test.

You will also want to keep your subjects separate. You can accomplish this by studying different subjects on separate days and even separate weeks, if you have enough time. Block your subjects and exercise sets into separate sections to help you establish a clear transition in your mind *before* the test. Studying is not just about reviewing or memorizing information. It is also about establishing good test habits weeks or even months before you walk into that room and sit down in front of the computer.

Mastering the MCAT

Do not allow your study plan to neglect the things that intimidate you. Many of the more science-minded students who take the MCAT may try to avoid studying for the verbal reasoning and writing sample sections because they may be intimidated by the writing component and the less-standardized nature of those parts of the test. This is a mistake. Avoiding these sections will not help you do better on the MCAT.

5. Execute your study plan

After a particularly dismal game during a losing season for the long-troubled Tampa Bay Buccaneers, then-coach John McKay was asked how he felt about his offense's execution. "I'm all for it," legend has it he responded. This play on words may also apply to your MCAT study plan, as you would probably like to paste it up in front of a firing squad more than you would like to carry out. However, only the latter form of execution is likely to help you gain admission to medical school. So once you have your plan in place, it is time to get to work.

You may be pleasantly surprised to find out how quickly you complete the tasks you have set out if you stick to your schedule. In any case, you should not hesitate to make changes to your plan as you study. You may find some topics to be more difficult than others, and they will therefore take longer to fully grasp than you may have anticipated. Or, if your review of the material goes quickly, you may have time for more practice tests. You may even decide to revise your overall target score based on how you are doing on practice tests.

As you work though practice problems, keep lists that will help you review as the test gets closer. For instance, you could keep a list of the concepts that are most difficult for you. Another list should contain the formulas that you might need on the test. The act of making the list will help you remember these formulas, and you will also be creating a handy study sheet.

Tip 22

Mastering the MCAT

Complex equations specific to the problem involved are often included on the test in the physical sciences and biological sciences sections. However, you cannot afford to assume that the equations you will need during the MCAT will be available on the test, or that you will be able to comprehend and use them without preparation and study beforehand. The only study materials that you can expect to have on the MCAT are the periodic table of the elements, scratch paper, and a pencil.

Grade yourself after each set of questions or practice test you take. Keep a record of both your times and your grades so that you can measure your study progress. You want to arrive at a time in your study where you finish sets or practice tests early, but still with the same grade as if you had finished at the time limit. You do not want to lose any points because you did not have enough time. This goes especially for the essays, in which a tough topic can bog you down. If you are organized, you can beat them.

Tip 23

Mastering the MCAT

Part of studying for the MCAT will be building up your mental endurance. While you can always take it again, nobody wants to do poorly or waste time taking the test repeatedly. This means that you must learn to concentrate. Study and practice the habits in this chapter as you would for the test. They will help you focus your concentration on the test and build up the mental endurance to tackle the MCAT.

chapter 04

Study Strategies

As you carry out your study plan, you should be employing a variety of strategies. Some will help you use your study time as effectively as possible. Other strategies will help you do your best on the test itself. It is important to practice these test-taking strategies before the test so that they become so ingrained, you will not even have to think about them on test day. After all, you will have enough to think about. Each person's method of studying will be unique because each test taker will have different strengths and weaknesses, goals, and preferences — not to mention that some will have more time to study than others. However, these simple strategies will help just about anyone as they prepare for the MCAT.

Master the Test Format

Each standardized test has its own rules and quirks. The best test takers exploit the structure of the test, taking advantage of such test specifics as how the questions are ordered and what types of questions each section contains. Here are some tips for making the most out of the MCAT's format.

CHICAGO HEIGHTS PUBLIC LIBRARY

Easiest questions first

As you complete practice tests, you will want to learn to take full advantage of the MCAT's format. One way to do that is to be sure that you are completing all of the easiest questions first. The MCAT, unlike some computerized tests, allows you to return to questions earlier in a section. Take advantage of that fact by passing over the most difficult questions until after you have completed the entire section. That way, you are sure to answer all of the easiest questions first.

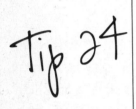

Mastering the MCAT

Be sure that you do all of the questions you know you can answer. Do not answer questions out of order, and do not linger on difficult questions. If a question is too confusing or difficult, make an educated guess and then move on. Jot down the numbers of the questions you guessed, or use the test's "mark" feature, as discussed in the previous chapter. You can always go back to them if you have the time.

If you concentrate on answering every question on the test too thoroughly, you may not have time to see all of the questions in that section, which means you might miss the chance to complete some easier questions toward the end. By making sure you get to choose the best ones to spend your time on, you will end up answering a higher number of easy questions and therefore, getting a higher score.

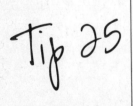

Mastering the MCAT

Remember that there is no penalty in the MCAT for a wrong answer. A wrong answer simply means that you will not get those points, not that you will be penalized extra points on top of that. So, answer away, even when you are not sure.

Another reason not to spend too much time on hard questions is that some questions that are deemed too difficult will not be included when the final, scaled score is determined for those who took that test. You will not know which of these questions will be disregarded in the scoring, so you cannot choose to skip them. However, you should try not to waste so much time on extremely difficult questions that you miss the chance to get the right answer on the easier questions.

Use the process of elimination

You should also use the MCAT's multiple-choice format to your advantage as you practice.

Three of the four sections of the MCAT, all but the writing section, are multiple choice. These questions may seem easy. After all, you are being given the answer. However, choosing which of the possible answers that you are given can be difficult, so it is best to practice working with this format before the test so that you are more adept at finding the right answer among the choices you are given.

Mastering the MCAT

Do not simply pick the answer that initially seems to be correct, as there often may be several that fall into that category. Choosing your answer too quickly may lead you to overlook other possible alternatives, including the right answer. Instead, narrow down the answers by eliminating the ones that are clearly not correct. Then, pick the one out of the remaining that is the most correct.

Sometimes, for instance, one answer will have accurate information, but will not completely answer the question you were given. That is to say, you want to pick the answer that is both complete and accurate. Do not pick an answer that seems partially or mostly correct. Some of the options may have part of the answer, but not as much as the one that is most correct.

Answer the question — only the question

The questions on the test may seem vague and confusing to you. Trust your instincts — they are intended to be that way. The MCAT is not intended to only be a test of your knowledge and abilities. Standardized tests are not generally straightforward at all. This increases the challenge and forces you to think about your responses, even though they are multiple-choice questions. The test makers intend to make you work for these answers.

This makes it doubly critical that you answer the question and only the question. Possibly the biggest mistake that you can make is to answer the subject rather than the question. What this means is that when you see the subject, you start to regurgitate the information that you know about it. You can do this even with a multiple-choice question when you see the question and your brain immediately brings up what you know. You then end up giving the answer that most closely matches what you reviewed and memorized instead of the one that answers the question.

Mastering the MCAT

To be sure you are choosing the answer to the exact question you are given — and not the one that seems to relate to the subject matter — you will need to read the question carefully. First, ask yourself what the subject is; then, ask yourself what the question is asking. Look at the answers and determine which ones answer the question. You often will see more than one possible correct answer. You will want to pick the one that answers the question most completely.

Follow the Test Rules

It is tempting to allow yourself plenty of leeway (extra time, study materials, and so on) as you take practice tests. If you take these shortcuts, however, you are giving up a crucial opportunity to practice the test in the same way you will experience it on test day. Following the test rules the whole time you study will make the actual test experience a habit, not a hardship, come test day.

Mastering the MCAT

When you do the exercises, use only the materials you will have available to you during the test so you do not learn to rely on materials you will not have access to. So, no books, no formula or other cheat sheets, and no calculators.

Keep the book closed

One rule you should always follow when you study is one of the most frustrating parts of the test: Don't turn to the resources available to help you along. Deal with this frustration up front instead of saving it for test day. The sooner you wean yourself off any crutches, the better off you will be in the test. You want to go into the testing center with correct expectations.

Obviously, there will be come questions that you simply cannot answer correctly without using books or other resources — that is why you are reviewing the material, right? But you should not just open your book immediately when you are in the middle of a practice test when you get stuck; you will not being able to do that during the actual MCAT. So, when you are doing the sample questions, treat that problem the same way you would on test day, even if that means eliminating a few answer choices and guessing. But do not give up on the question entirely. After you have gone through each question in a set this way, go back and solve them using whatever resources you can and as much time as it takes.

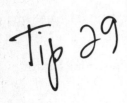

Mastering the MCAT

Use books and other resources to help you through problems only after you have tried each problem at least once as you would see it on test day: without books or other help, and with limited time to complete it.

Time yourself

Time is a major issue on the MCAT, and it should play a big role in your study habits, too. You have already carved out the time to study, so break out your stopwatch and keep time in the forefront as you complete practice tests and exercises, too. This way, you know how much time you are taking to answer questions and can narrow down your time to be within the testing limits.

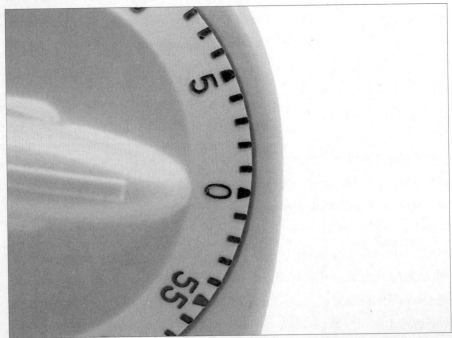

Mastering the MCAT

Give yourself the same amount of time for a set of exercises that you will get during the test: about 80 seconds a question for the two science-based sections, and 90 seconds for the verbal reasoning section.

If you are able to practice to the point where you can complete all of the questions in each section within the time limit, you will lessen your anxiety about not finishing in time. Even if you had to guess on a few questions, your score will improve because you have had enough time to see and consider each question. Ideally, you should then spend most of that time on the ones you have the greatest chance of answering correctly.

Mastering the MCAT

You can always go back within that section if you reach the end of it with time to spare and have a brainstorm. Often, being a few minutes away from a particular question will help you approach it with a new, sometimes better, perspective.

Pay attention to how much time you can spend on individual questions. If you know how much time you should be spending, on average, on each question, this will keep you from lingering on hard questions and move on to questions you can answer. Remember that you do not have a lot of time in the test to spend on the more difficult questions. As such, you really need to watch that you do not get bogged down in them. Give yourself 45 seconds to set up a multiple-choice problem, so that the rest of your 80 seconds can be devoted to actually solving it. If you cannot get a handle on how to approach a question in that time, you should probably guess and move on because you likely will not be able to complete it within 80 seconds.

Finally, to get the most out of your timing practice, do not break up exercise sets; you will get these sets all together during the test. This will help you learn to concentrate on quickly absorbing the information given for each set and doing each set as a unit.

Mastering the MCAT

The questions in each set all come from the same experiment or reading and are therefore related to each other. Answering them separately is more likely to lower your score than to raise it.

Recreate the test environment

Beyond the actual test rules, you will want to get used to the other quirks of the standardized testing environment, some comfortable and some not so comfortable. After all, lounging with your laptop on your thighs and textbooks surrounding you is not quite what the MCAT will be like, so studying that way is not the best preparation. As much as possible, you should make your study environment the same as it will be in the testing area when you take the MCAT.

Mastering the MCAT

Complete the practice exercises sitting in a chair at a desk or table rather then on a bed or couch. Turn off the television and radio. Do not go on the Internet or have it available while doing a set of exercises. If you find this difficult to do, sit in a room without a computer. Turn off your cell phone. None of these things will be present while you are taking the test.

While you want to create a quiet setting like the one in which you will take the test for your study sessions, you do not want to become too dependent on utter silence to get through the MCAT questions. After all, interruptions will happen during your test. People will cough, sneeze, sigh, and clear their throats. If you always study in absolute silence, you will not be prepared for these kinds of interruptions, so you will want to do some studying with these minor irritations present.

Tip 34

Mastering the MCAT

Once you have established a distraction-free routine, try scheduling in some interruptions, perhaps by practicing in a public place like the library. Remember to time and grade these sets just as you do the regular sessions. You need to assure yourself those interruptions will not interfere with your pace or score.

Take breaks

When you take the MCAT, you will be allowed to take a ten-minute break between each of the four sections. If you do not take these breaks, you can simply continue with the test. This might be tempting, but these breaks provide you with a brief respite between sections to clear your head and switch your concentration between sections. You do not have to take them, but you should — both on the actual test and when you practice. Take your ten minutes to walk around, stretch your legs, have a snack, or just pop in a peppermint to boost your alertness. You will not receive extra credit for toughing it out, and if you try to do so, your score is likely to suffer accordingly.

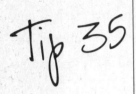

Mastering the MCAT

Do not make the mistake of eschewing breaks because you feel you do not need them. The MCAT is long and grueling. Exhaustion can creep up on you before you know it. By the time you realize that you are in trouble, you may not have any breaks in order to catch up on your energy level.

Prepare physically

The MCAT is a physical challenge as well as a mental one. In that long stretch in front of the computer, you might deal with eyestrain, back pain, hunger, and other physical distractions that might derail your test-taking efforts. All too often, students tell themselves that it is not necessary to physically prepare for a mental challenge, even though your physical condition greatly affects your mental condition. Just as you would want to take care of your body before a marathon, you also need to take care of your health before the MCAT. Get regular exercise, sleep for eight hours every night, and eat well in the months and weeks leading up to the test so that you will be able to handle the physical challenge of taking the test.

Mastering the MCAT

Figure out during your study periods where you become tired and where you have the most energy in the test. Then flag those areas when you are practicing. This will be beneficial to you because it allows you to balance out your efforts accordingly.

Another part of preparing physically for the test is building up your endurance so that you are able to concentrate for the duration of the test. You can do this by making sure at least some, but not all, of your study sessions are five to six hours long. Try mixing shorter sessions of two or three hours with half a dozen or so longer, five- to six-hour sessions. During those sessions, stay focused on the test throughout the session, except for the breaks outlined above.

Tip 37

Mastering the MCAT

Longer study sessions will allow you to build up your test endurance — your ability to handle both the physical discomfort of sitting at a computer that long and the need to concentrate the entire time.

Manage test anxiety

Anxiety affects many students. Some may have no difficulty with their studies or class exams but freeze up on major exams like the MCAT. The obstacles for such students are the test itself and how highly they value the outcome. Such anxiety may seem overwhelming sometimes, but you can overcome it, and you will need to learn how to do so if you want to pass the MCAT.

Part of what is being tested in the MCAT is your ability to work past your anxiety and stress and perform under pressure. Besides, that is what you are going to be doing every day as a medical student and, eventually, a health care professional.

The most effective way to beat test anxiety is to prepare for the test, particularly by doing full-length simulated tests. After a few of these simulations, the act of taking the test feels routine, not strange, and that will keep at bay the part of test anxiety that is triggered by unfamiliar situations. Being prepared will also kill some of those "I am going to do horribly" demons. You can also reduce stress by being prepared in small ways: Get a good night's sleep, gather your supplies the day before, and so on.

Finally, consider limiting your contact with other test takers at the testing site. You may think a little conversation will be relaxing, but conversation can be unpredictable. You never know what another person might say, quite innocently, that will send off anxiety alarms in the crucial minutes before you take the test.

Do not wait until the test is in front you to figure out how to relax in the face of stress and anxiety. When you are a practicing medical professional, you will need to be able to relax in any situation, so you might as well start practicing relaxation now.

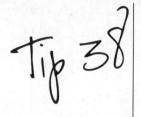

Mastering the MCAT

Stop and stretch or breathe deeply when you start to feel stressed during your study sessions so that you will remember to do that during the test, too.

The following Web site, set up by a University of South Florida professor as part of the College of Education, can help you find out more information about relaxation techniques during studying and tests: **www. coedu.usf.edu/zalaquett/Help_Screens/Relaxation.htm**. Some basic exercises include:

- Stretching your arms above your head, hands clasped together, three to five times during the test.

- Rolling your chin along your chest from shoulder to the other three times in a row.

- Tucking your chin to your chest to stretch your vertebrae in the back of your neck. Do this for half a minute three to five times during the test.

- Drawing a breath in slowly, holding it for five counts, and then letting it out. Do this ten to 50 times in a row, depending on your stress level and the time available. Remember to breathe deeply during the other exercises, as well.

Know yourself

No one study plan will work best for everyone who plans to take the MCAT. Some people will need to study different topic areas more than others, for instance, and some will need to devote more of their energy to managing test anxiety. To maximize your performance on the MCAT, get to know your own habits and preferences on everything from when to take the test to how to study for what is on it.

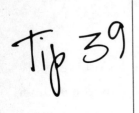

Mastering the MCAT

Schedule your MCAT during a time of day that best suits your own body clock. There is no point in handicapping yourself by choosing an afternoon test time when you are a morning person, or an early morning test if you are a night owl. The time to change your sleep schedule is not the day that you take the MCAT.

Certain sections will test your ability to deal with anxiety more than others. For the many science-centered people who take the test, for instance, the verbal reasoning section and writing sections might get their heart beating faster than any physics problem. Know which parts of the test stress you out the most so you can mentally prepare for those parts on test day. If biological science gets you flustered, work on ways to overcome your anxiety and put in your best performance on that section. If your performance is a little rough on these sections, do not let it bring you down.

Mastering the MCAT

Just concentrate on studying if you find yourself stuck on sections so that your performance is complete and competent. The more time you spend mastering those sections, the less anxious you are likely to be when you encounter them during the actual test.

Expect the unexpected

When you read about the test or go through the questions, do you ever get the idea that the testers are deliberately trying to trip you up — that they want to make you work harder, want to tire you out, want to make you fail? If you do, you are right. They want to make you work harder than if you were taking a normal college test. This is their job, and the job of the test.

The test is not there simply to test your skills or your knowledge in science and logic; it is also there to test your skills in dealing with unexpected and unfamiliar situations. This is why you do not get any extra time or consideration for interruptions during the test — though you do for handicaps, as these would be accommodated in medical school, as well. It is why the questions often seem unnecessarily confusing or overly complex, and why you never seem to have quite enough time. They are intentionally set up that way to test your ability to solve problems under fire. So no matter how much you study, you should also prepare yourself for the possibility of finding something completely new come test day.

Mastering the MCAT

Expect questions that you did not anticipate, subjects that your question sets and practice tests did not cover, and interruptions that you did not expect. If you come to terms with these things before the test, and learn to expect them on test day, they will not affect your concentration or derail your confidence.

chapter | *05*

Countdown to Test Day

Y ou do not want to find out the day before the test about the things you should have been doing in the months and weeks leading up to it. To make sure this does not happen to you, here is a countdown of what you should be doing from the time you first start studying to the day of the test itself.

The Months Before the Test

You should consider when you need to take the test and how you will study for it, well before you actually register for the MCAT. For one thing, if you have not completed or mastered the basic premed coursework, you may need to complete college courses or other intensive reviews in the relevant subject areas, which cannot be done in just a few months. At the very least, you will want plenty of time to get used to the test format and brush up on your weak areas.

As discussed in the book so far, you should devote part of your time to studying for the MCAT during the months (or even a year or more) leading up to the test. This will include the steps of setting goals, gathering your study materials, developing a study plan, and implementing that plan. If you find that you are still struggling in one or more of the content areas that will be covered on the test, consider signing up for a class or hiring an experienced tutor a few months before the test. Do not wait until the last minute to get help. If you do poorly in one area, for example, then you may need extra work in that area. If you do consistently well in that area, you should consider that subject sufficiently reviewed and move on to a subject that could use more attention.

Mastering the MCAT

Do practice questions and exams at all points of your study progression, from the very first day to the week before the test. Doing this will help you familiarize yourself with the MCAT test early on. It will also help you measure your progress, which will reassure you about where you are in your review and reorient your direction of study if it goes off course.

As you study during the months leading up to the test, you should be building your test stamina and physically preparing for the test by periodically taking full-length MCAT practice tests. Try to schedule these practice tests for the time of day when you will take the actual test so that you can develop a routine for waking up, eating, and doing other activities that you will do on test day.

As you get closer to test day, the way you study should also be changing. Rather than setting out to study for the entire test, as you did in the beginning, you should be narrowing down the list of concepts to which you need to devote further study. By two months before the test, for instance, you should have crossed off more than half of the list of topics covered in the "Inside the MCAT" chapter of this book. *See Chapter 2 for this section.* These would be the ones that you have already studied and mastered. The topics you have left to study in the final months, or at least the last two weeks, should be ones that you have reviewed once but still feel you need to work on more before test day.

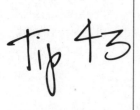

Mastering the MCAT

As the test gets closer, make sure you are on track to review all of the material on the test at least a few weeks before test day so you can spend extra time in your weak areas right before the test.

If you need more help

At some point, you may realize that you would like the extra help and moral support that comes with studying in a group or with a paid tutor. If you choose to hire a tutor, do so at least a few weeks before the test, so that you will have time to work through all of the concepts that are troubling you. And be prepared: A good MCAT tutor could cost you up to $100 an hour.

There is nothing wrong with getting more help at the beginning of your review period to augment your study, but you can get the most out of any outside help by doing your homework first. Make sure you have tried your best to understand each concept before you ask a tutor or study partner to help. That way, you will be more likely to understand his or her explanation — and you would not be paying someone to do what you could have done yourself. Show up at a study group with specific questions, not a declaration of "I don't get it." No one can do your studying for you, especially in an area that involves so much memorization of formulas, equations, and rules as chemistry and physics.

Mastering the MCAT

Come into any study group situation prepared. People will be much happier to help if they see that you have studied first and are only asking questions about subjects you genuinely do not understand. A systematic approach will make more efficient use of your study time and energy.

Another way to organize your study is to audit a 1000-level college class. Auditing allows you to sit in on the lectures but does not generally require you to take the tests or the labs, and it does not count as a grade. Sitting in on these classes will allow you to hear the material explained by experienced professors, which is an effective form of review. However, you should avoid sitting in on any class for free without permission. Most universities have policies against this. Plus, key faculty members teach many 1000-level courses, so if you try to audit a class without permission, you risk offending the people you may need as references in that subject.

You can also use an AP (advanced placement) syllabus or outline to organize your test subjects. Though taken in high school, AP tests are intended to replace college 1000-level courses and represent a condensation of the topics needed for such a course. Because students are taking the AP course in high school or even on their own, the AP can be a good model for a relatively short course in the study of the necessary material that you need to know in a freshman-level course. Course descriptions can be found online at CollegeBoard (**http://apcentral.collegeboard.com**).

Register for the test

You will also want to register at least two months in advance of the test date to make sure that you get the date and time that you want. To register online, go to AAMC Web site (**www.aamc.org/students/mcat/reserving/ start.htm**), and create a username and password. At the time you register, you should also consider these factors:

- Enter your name in the registration form in the exact same way that it appears on the identification (usually your driver's license) you will use on test day. For most people, that will be their full name, but if your ID only has a middle initial, then register that way.

- Double-check your registration to make sure you have the right time and location of the test. Mark your calendar with the appropriate time.

- Make sure that your schedule is clear for the entire day of the test so that you will not have other commitments competing with the test for your attention. Make sure to make arrangements for babysitting and to have time off from work. While you are at it, go ahead and print out directions to the facility and the actual room where you will take the test.

These items may seem trivial, but they reflect the administrative worries that many test takers have. Worries interfere with your concentration and slow you down during the test. If you make arrangements and confirm them beforehand, you will not have these worries and will enter the testing center on the day of your exam with a clear mind.

The Week Before the Test

Students commonly make poor decisions while studying for tests of any kind. One of those is cramming at the last minute, including the night before and right up until the moment before the test. This is not a healthy way to go about preparing for a test (especially the MCAT) and will often leave students exhausted and unable to concentrate on test day. Even worse, excessive studying that leads you to lose sleep in the week before the test could make you vulnerable to some nasty bug going around town, leaving you sick on test day.

Mastering the MCAT

As you make your final preparations, you should be focused more on your physical well being than on last-minute study. Think about what you would do if you intended to run a marathon. Would you never practice but expect to excel on race day? Would you eat poorly, sleep little, abuse drugs, or drink alcohol? Would you come into the marathon the day of the race having run all night to get into shape at the last minute? Of course not.

Just as you would physically prepare for a race months beforehand, you should prepare for the MCAT well in advance of test day. Then, as the test approaches, focus on making sure that you feel good both mentally and physically. In addition, you should be completing frequent, short study sessions to keep your test-taking muscles (namely your brain) in shape. These sessions should focus on the parts of the test that are most difficult for you.

About a week before the test, you should take the following steps:

- Take one more full-length practice test.

- Narrow down your study list to ten or fewer concepts with which you still are not completely comfortable. Keep a list of these topics as you study, and narrow down the list as test day approaches. Make sure that you are not saving any new material for the last week before the test.

- Pull together the list of formulas and solutions to common question types that you have been keeping throughout the course. If it is in a rough draft, re-write or type it so that it will be easier to study as the test approaches.

- Set aside at least an hour every day before the test to study for the MCAT.

- Log on to the AAMC Web site and make sure that all of your registration is complete, on record, and paid for. If you have made any special arrangements (for any disability, temporary, or otherwise), confirm that these have been finalized and that the testing center is aware of them.

- Check to make sure you have a current driver's license or passport to use as identification. An expired form of ID will not be accepted. When you log on to the AAMC site to check your registration, make sure your name appears exactly the same on the ID you will use and on your test registration.

- Buy any supplies you might need for the test. If you do not keep healthy, non-perishable snacks on hand, pick some of these up. If you concerned about noise, buy some earplugs; these are allowed in the testing room.

- Visit your testing site to make sure you know how to find the location, including the room where the test will be administered.

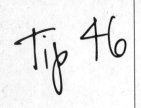

Mastering the MCAT

You should allot your study time during the final week for reviewing the concepts that you still need to work on and your list of formulas and solutions to common problems. You should not be reviewing new material because you will not have time to master it in the last week.

The Night Before the Test

The night before the test is the perfect time to cram in an extra five to eight hours of study, right? Wrong. If you have followed this advice so far, you have done plenty of studying in the weeks and months leading up to the test, and you are as ready as you are going to be. On the night before, your best bet is to take care of yourself and make sure you have all the details covered so that test day will be stress-free.

- Get a good night's sleep (at least eight hours). Try to do this the entire week before the test if you can so that you will be in top physical condition.

- Eat a large, healthy meal the night before the test — enough food to help you sleep well, but not fatty or heavily spiced food that will give you indigestion on test day.

- Do something pleasant and distracting the night before. Rent a movie or watch a favorite TV show. It may seem like a good idea to think about only the test, but your mind can only concentrate for so long.

- If your urge to study is strong, spend no more than an hour lightly reviewing some test content. Run over your list of formulas, focusing on the ones that are hardest to memorize, or review a question that you found particularly difficult to remind yourself how to solve such a problem. Doing this will help you reassure yourself that you have adequately prepared for the test, making you feel more relaxed and confident.

- Avoid heavy studying. A long study session will rob you of sleep, which is far more important at this stage in the game than the little bit of material you can memorize in one night.

- Pack a bag with everything you will bring to the test, including your registration and ID. You should also pack directions to the test site, layers of clothing (in case the room is cold or hot), and a non-perishable, healthy snack such as a granola bar to eat during a break. You may want to bring along an MP3 player to listen to or a book to read for a few minutes before the test if you arrive early; you can then stow them in the lockers provided before you go in to the test. Make note of any perishable items, such as a piece of fruit or a cold bottle of water or sports drink, that you will need to add to your supplies right before you leave for the test.

- Read through the "MCAT Essentials" document that will be provided to you by AAMC when you register. Read the "MCAT Examinee Agreement" in the back of this document that you will have to agree to on test day. It will not change, and by reading it in advance, you will not have to read it before the actual test. This will make your overall testing time shorter, thereby cutting down on test fatigue.

The Morning of the Test

On test day, you do not want to start thinking about the MCAT half an hour before it is time to leave the house, nor do you want to spend the entire day of the test focused solely on MCAT material. Instead, you want to strike a balance so that you are completely prepared in advance, but still have a little time to unwind with more relaxing activities. Here are some test-day tips to help you make sure you are at your best when the timer starts ticking:

- Get up at least two hours ahead of when you need to leave. This will give you plenty of time to get ready and to deal with any last-minute disasters that may arise despite your careful planning, whether it is finding someone to care for a sick child or fixing a flat tire.

- Do not sweat the small stuff. You do not need to show up fashion-ably dressed. This is a major standardized test; no one will care. Also leave yourself plenty of time to get to the test. Twice as much time as you think you need is a good benchmark, especially if you are using public transportation or anticipate traffic. Do not procrastinate.

- A good meal in the morning, such as cereal and fruit, is also a good idea because it will give you extra energy. If you do not eat in the morning, your energy may flag halfway through the test. On the other hand, you do not want to have a heavy breakfast because it may make you feel tired. However, some people may have difficulty with eating before a test as their anxiety makes them nauseous. Play this one by ear; only you know your body.

- Show up at least 45 minutes before the test. Testing sites may change location at the last minute, so you may arrive at the wrong place. Plan ahead for these things so you do not arrive in a panic or flustered.

Giving yourself so much time on the day before the test may seem coun-terproductive if you are trying to get a good night's sleep, but it does two things. First, it gives you plenty of time to calm down and mentally prepare for the test if you are nervous. Second, it gives you plenty of time and space in which to deal with any last-minute issues that might affect your test score. Remember that the test center will not allow you extra time if you are distracted or derailed. If you go in prepared, this will reduce your anxiety and reduce the likelihood of anything unforeseen shaking your focus. Be kind to yourself: Making things harder for yourself will not improve your score.

At the Testing Site

As noted, you must arrive at the testing center at least 30 minutes before your test is scheduled to start, though getting there even earlier is preferable. If staff is not ready to check you in once you arrive early, you can spend a few minutes reading or otherwise relaxing until it is time to get ready for the test.

Once you are at the site, you will want to be sure you store all of your belongings in the lockers provided. You will not be allowed to bring any testing materials such as pencils or scratch paper into the test area; these will be provided for you. In fact, you will only be allowed to take in your personal clothing, which you must keep on at all times or store in the facility's lockers. You may not even bring in a hat, and you certainly are not allowed any cell phones or pagers, which must be turned off even in storage.

The testing staff will admit test takers one at a time into the testing room, so be prepared to wait your turn before you start taking the test. Staff at the testing site will check your identification, take your fingerprints, and assign you a computer workstation. You may not pick your own workstation. While you do not want to delay the process of getting settled, do not be afraid to ask any questions about the testing site or procedures.

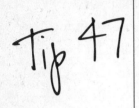

Mastering the MCAT

The clock will not stop on your test if you are required to leave the test area to rectify any of these issues, so be sure you understand the rules and follow them. You would not want to lose precious minutes of test time putting your hat in a locker should the proctor miss it on the way in. If you show up late or without the proper ID, you will have to reschedule for another date.

During the test

Studying will help you concentrate on the strategies and subjects needed to prepare for the test. However, there are some strategies that you will need to keep in mind at the most crucial moment of all: once the actual test starts. While you may have worked through some of these while you were taking practices, consider writing these goals down quickly on your scratch paper once you get to the test; this will clear your head for answering the questions, as well as remind you of each goal.

1. Live in the moment

Do not think about the previous section once you have gone on to the next one, no matter how well (or poorly) you think you did. This will only hurt your concentration on the task at hand: your current section. You also do not want to spend time thinking about any sections coming up, either. It is easy, for example, to find the verbal reasoning and writing sample sections highly intimidating — or at least a major switch in gears from the more precise science sections. But you will only hurt yourself by trying to psych yourself up for these sections beforehand. Study for them, but during the actual test, go in cold from the previous section.

2. Pace yourself

Just as in your study periods, pacing yourself comes into play during the test. You should be aware of how much time you have left for each section and how many questions remain — you will have a timer on your screen to help you keep track of your time on each question and for the entire section. On average, you will have about one-and-a-quarter minutes for each science question, and a minute and a half for each reading question — though some of the easier questions in all sections should be answered more quickly. Do not get lost in solving the question and forgetting about the rest of your test. As a general rule, if you have spent 30 seconds on a question and still are not sure you are on your way to finding the answer, you should consider marking it and moving onto another question. Also, keep in mind that the tough biological sciences section, with its emphasis on organic chemistry, comes after the verbal reasoning and writing sample sections, which may tire you out. Pace yourself so that does not happen.

3. Avoid getting stuck

Be wary of getting stuck on one question or question set. Do not become seduced by the concept of the perfect score. Very few people actually achieve a 45T on the MCAT — in fact, AAMC reported that no one received a perfect score in 2009, and the highest score was a 42T, with only 0.1 percent of test takers achieving that score. Simply put: You do not need a perfect score in order to do well on the MCAT. What you need is a *good* score. To get that, you will need to move on to a new question rather than fret when one is not going well. A good rule of thumb is that if you are not on your way to the right answer in 30 seconds, you should guess and move on. Similarly, you have started to work through a problem but hit a wall after a minute, move on. You can mark that question and come back to it later if you have time.

While you do not want to go through the test too slowly, you also do not want to panic and rush through the test too quickly. Even reading passages in the verbal reasoning section of the MCAT are not that long and are meant to be able to be read within the time allotted. You will want to proceed through the entire test at a steady pace. If you finish some questions more quickly than others, that is great but have an upper limit for how much time you spend on any question before moving on. Remember that the MCAT is a marathon, not a sprint.

4. Relax

You should have already practiced some relaxation techniques as you studied for the test. Now, it is time to employ them on test day. The best relaxation techniques for the test are those that allow you to stretch and breathe deeply while sitting. You will not be allowed to stand up and walk around except during your breaks. There are many stretching and breathing exercises that do not involve standing up. *Reference back to Chapter 4 for a few ideas.* Breathing exercises in particular can help regulate anxiety, which is something that may plague you when you are running low on time and start to worry that you will not finish.

5. Do not void your scores

Once you have completed the test, you will be given an option to either score or void your exam. If you choose to void it, your exam will not be graded, which means you will never know how well you did on that test, nor will you be given a refund. This option may be tempting to some test takers, but very few people would actually benefit from such a move.

Mastering the MCAT

Do not give in to the temptation to void your test scores simply because you do not feel you did your very best. It will be better for you in the long run to know how you did so that you can better prepare for the next test. You should void your test only if you did not complete large parts of it for some unexpected reason.

Once the Test is Over

For the vast majority of people who take the MCAT, the final step after taking the test will be to check in for their scores. Some people, however, will leave the test with lingering issues that must be addressed. Here is how you should go about tying up loose ends after the test:

- To find out your score, log on to the AAMC Web site 30–35 days after you take the test. You should receive a more precise estimated date when your results would be ready when you register.

- Once you have checked your scores, you can register for another test if you feel you need to try again. Be sure to give yourself enough time to study appropriately before taking the test again; otherwise, your score is unlikely to improve much.

- If you experienced a problem at the testing center that caused you not to take the test on your scheduled day, you can log on to the AAMC Web site within 48 hours of your original test date to register for a new test, though you will have to pay for the new test. These problems could range from missing the test altogether to having an expired or improper ID.

- If you have a concern about the way your test was administered and would like AAMC to research this issue, you must take two steps: First, submit a Center Problem Report with the test center administrator. Second, notify AAMC of your concerns. You should also contact the MCAT testing office within five days of taking the test if you feel a particular question was unfair.

chapter | 06

The Science Sections

F ace it: Much of what you are going to be studying, and stressing over, are the two science sections, physical sciences and biological sciences, which will cover anything and everything from atomic theory to zoology. Later chapters on each section will detail the concepts covered in each section, including the relevant definitions and formulas. For now, we will cover some material and strategies that are useful for both science sections.

Format and Strategy

The physical sciences and biological sciences sections each contain 52 questions that must be completed in 70 minutes. Each section is broken up into several sets of questions based on a particular passage or issue. Each passage will have seven to nine questions. In addition, each section will include 10–13 freestanding questions outside of the question sets.

As is the case for all of the MCAT (except the writing section), you will be graded on a scale from one to 15 for each section, with your overall grade for the section scaled against others' scores. Questions will be weighted based on the levels of difficulty, with more difficult questions receiving more weight than easier questions. In addition, not every question is included in your final grade. Some questions were put on the test for experimental purposes to try them out for possible use in future tests. Others will be thrown out because they created problems for scaling and usually because too few students answered them correctly.

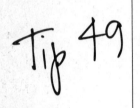

Mastering the MCAT

You will not be able to determine until after the test which questions will not be graded, so answer all of them. Remember that there are no penalties for incorrect answers, so your grade will not suffer regardless, as long as you answer all of the questions that you can within your allotted time.

You can improve your score greatly in both science sections by completing practice sets — then completing more practice tests. These will help you become more comfortable with the test structure and what will be expected of you. *You will find some exercise sets at the end of each chapter in Part II devoted to the four sections of the test.* You will also find online resources for practice tests in the back of this book.

Types of questions

You are only required to apply basic scientific principles to solve the problems in the physical and biological science sections. You are not required to know either calculus or string theory to pass the MCAT. Although the two science sections are roughly divided into physics, biology, and chemistry questions, you will see among between all three areas: A chemistry or physics question may well include biological elements.

Mastering the MCAT

The MCAT test is intended to test your knowledge of medicine-related concepts, not any one particular discipline. If you go into the test expecting to see question sets that address more than one scientific discipline at once, you will find them easier to deal with. Falsely expecting only neatly divided problems will quickly get you into trouble, so make sure you prepare yourself for all types of questions and scenarios.

The questions in these sections of the test will all involve basic scientific principles that you would encounter in freshman science courses with labs. The questions will test your knowledge of these basic scientific concepts, as well as your overall ability to solve complex problems. While the question sets may give you a great deal of detail, you will already have the information that you *need* to answer the questions. Study the basic concepts and the equations related to them, and let the question sets give you the rest. The science sections have four basic types of questions: reasoning questions, problem-solving questions, experiment-based questions, and evidentiary questions.

Reasoning questions: These are questions that involve information you do not know and are not meant to know in advance. They are intended to test your reasoning skills when faced with new information. The questions often revolve around an experimental approach to a familiar subject and may involve complex graphs or diagrams that may confuse you at first glance.

Mastering the MCAT

Reasoning questions are one part of the test where your scratch paper becomes useful. To make sense of these difficult questions, draw the graph or diagram out so that you have it in front of you. This will keep it straight in your head and help you work your way to a solution.

Problem-solving questions: These are somewhat like reasoning questions because they involve reasoning your way to a solution based on information you may not already have rather than using your own knowledge set. These may involve solving a problem using an equation, but more often, they involve solving a problem outlined in the passage using your knowledge of basic scientific concepts. The MCAT tries to avoid crunching numbers, preferring instead to test actual scientific knowledge.

Experiment-based questions: These are question sets based around a particular experiment that is outlined in the passage. You will usually get the results of the experiment as a graph or in a table. The question might ask you to evaluate the conclusions made in the passage, the way the experiment was set up, or the way the data was collected. For example, the question may ask if the method of collection contaminated the conclusions or whether the conclusions support the original question.

Mastering the MCAT

Most often, experiment-based questions are about the structure and validity of the experiment, not the statistical results. Do not get bogged down in the details. Remember that this is about solving the problem, not doing calculations.

Evidentiary questions: These questions will give you a set of information and then ask you to draw and evaluate conclusions about it. These questions are about testing an argument to determine whether it is weak or strong. As with the other question types, these questions will be founded on basic scientific principles, no matter how vague they appear at first glance.

Taking questions in order

Opinions vary over whether you should take questions in the order they come or whether you should skip around, and both sides have merit. If you skip around, you will be sure to answer all the questions you know how to solve without running out of time at the end; however, you might get confused with all the skipping around or waste time going back and forth between questions. On the other hand, if you go in order, you run the risk of spending a lot of time on early questions and never seeing other questions at the end that could be easier for you.

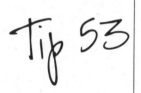

Mastering the MCAT

Whether to skip around is a judgment call on your part. Experiment doing this different ways as you do practice tests and decide on the best approach well before the test day. No matter what you choose, you should do sets as complete units. You do not want to get stuck on a difficult question, but you do not want to get confused and lose your place, either. You should therefore at least skim over each question in order.

If a question is too difficult and you cannot make an educated guess, mark it and move on. If you have enough time to come back to it at the end of the question set or section (as you should, if you have planned out your breaks sufficiently), look at it again. Having answered the easier questions, you may now have a better idea of how this question fits into the overall set.

Mastering the MCAT

Do not leave a question unanswered when going through the section. You may not have time to return to it, so it is best to put something down. Be sure to mark the questions that you guess on so that you will know which ones to try again if you have time.

Reading the passages

There are two possible methods of reading the passage. The first is to read through the passage carefully; the second is to skim it multiple times. How do you determine which is the best one? As you did when deciding how to answer the questions, practice both methods while studying for the test. This is part of familiarizing yourself with the test but also of familiarizing yourself with your individual responses to the test. Use the practice sets and practice tests to determine which method works best for you. You should not wait until the middle of the MCAT test to explore which method you prefer.

In the first method, read through the passage from beginning to end. Make brief notes as you do on your scratch pad. Note especially the main idea and the main arguments. If this is an experiment, ask yourself some key questions: What is the purpose of the experiment? What is the underlying hypothesis? If this is an evidentiary question set, ask yourself what scientific concept is being covered and what is being said about it. If this is a problem-solving question set, ask yourself what problem is being solved and in what scientific field. By doing this, you gather a solid understanding of the overall point of the passage on the first reading that you can then apply to the questions. This is a good method to use if you are generally strong in reading comprehension.

In the second method, do multiple scans and use each scan to pick up a different type of information. On the first scan, ask yourself what type of question set this is: reasoning, problem solving, experiment based, or evidentiary. On the second scan, ask yourself what scientific discipline is being covered. Does the question set cover more than one discipline? If so, how many and which ones? On the third pass, ask yourself what the main idea is — in other words, what is the experiment, information, problem, or piece of evidence the question revolves around? This is a good method to use if you have a hard time internalizing the content you read because it provides your reading with a more set structure.

Mastering the MCAT

If you choose to use this multiple-scan method, it may help to write down the answers to each question as you scan the passage. That way, you will have some key words in front of you as you try to answer the question. For instance, if you read through the passage three times as mentioned above, you might write down "reasoning, physics/chemistry, thermodynamics." As you work the question, your mind will be searching for information that relates to these topics. In addition, you will remember to employ the correct strategy for reasoning questions.

Now look at the questions themselves. Question sets will usually begin with general questions and move into more specific questions as the set goes on. Freestanding questions are likely to be fairly general because they do not have a passage on which to draw. It may also be helpful to read the questions first before you read the entire passage, particularly if you are intimidated by the content of the passage, because it allows you to focus on the parts of the passage that are being asked about in the questions rather than wasting time on difficult content that is not tested. If you do so, avoid becoming so focused on any one question that you forget about the passage and the other questions.

As you can see, each method gains you the same information, but in different ways. Determine which method is best for you by trying each one out on several question sets. Pick the one that gives you the highest score and the best time. Keep in mind that different methods may work on different types of question sets. The best way to prevail on the MCAT is to keep your thoughts organized while remaining flexible. Every student is a little different in this respect, so find out what kind of student you are. Even if you are sure that you will prefer one method to another, take the time during your study to confirm this.

Mastering the MCAT

Do not try to memorize information within the passage or set; instead use figures or graphs as resources. Do not feel that you need to understand or know all of the information in a graph, chart, or figure — only what you need in order to answer the questions. This may seem obvious, but consider that most premed students taking the MCAT have spent the past four years absorbing information so that they can do well on this final exam. You do not want to remain stuck in that mindset when taking the MCAT.

Always focus on the scientific concept used in the passage or question. You do not need to employ creative problem solving; only concentrate on the fundamental concept underlying the passage and answer the questions. This knowledge may include essential equations or formulas. You do not have time to learn new information from the passage in the time you are allotted. Instead, you have just enough time to identify any pertinent concepts that you have memorized, deal with any new information in the passage, and use it to answer the questions.

Remember why you are being tested

Keep in mind the purpose of this test: You are trying to get into medical school, so you will be tested on scientific concepts that are relevant to the medical field. You may see some unrelated subjects in the verbal reasoning section, but the science sections will only involve medical-related material. The medical field sees considerable overlap between disciplines within the diagnosis and treatment of a single problem or patient illness. If you try to think in an interdisciplinary manner like a physician, you will have an easier time answering these questions. As a practicing doctor will likely do, you will need to skim the material for the most important information.

Mastering the MCAT

You will not be graded on how well you read or comprehend the passages, but on how correctly you answer the questions. That is all. Always focus on getting through your reading in time to answer the questions. This goes for all three of the multiple-choice sections of the test.

Studying for the Sciences Sections

When studying for the science sections, study the fundamentals first. In textbooks, you can find the fundamental concepts of a subject at the beginning of each chapter and in a recap at the end (you may also see overviews and recaps for individual sections). Write down any equations that are featured in general overviews of a topic before you delve into more detailed material. These are the most important and fundamental equations and concepts within that subject, which is why they appear in the overviews and recaps. Do this for all of the subjects within a discipline before moving on to the next one.

Mastering the MCAT

Once you have reviewed the basics, you can move on to the more complex concepts, which are found in the latter part of each chapter in most textbooks.

You will be accomplishing two things with this studying technique. First, should you run short of time near the end of your studies, you still would have reviewed all of your subjects on at least the basic level. Remember that the MCAT tests you both on your knowledge of these subjects and how you handle new information using the information you already have. If you know all of the basics, you can still make an educated guess, even if the question is more advanced than what you have previously reviewed. If you review all the details of one concept but get more questions regarding the concepts you did not review, you will not do as well if you had reviewed all subjects at the same basic level.

Second, it means that you can answer interdisciplinary questions more readily. Remember that these concepts often overlap, and if you have fully reviewed the fundamental concepts in all of those disciplines, you can figure out the more complex questions with the knowledge you have gained and some common sense. Once you have reviewed your materials, you may still encounter questions or areas where you feel puzzled or weak. This is a good time to go online and ask for help on a board for premed or medical students, or ask your fellow premed students.

Mathematics content

The MCAT does not test math in a separate section, but you will need to know some basic math concepts in order to answer certain questions in both the science chapters. You need not recall all the most advanced calculus concepts you have ever learned, however; instead, much of the math you will see on the MCAT is made up of fairly simple arithmetic such as proportions and percentages, as well as more advanced topics you may have learned in courses such as statistics and geometry. The following is a list of the mathematics concepts you will need to be familiar with in order to complete all MCAT questions successfully.

Arithmetic

Perhaps the majority of the math you will use on the MCAT is fairly simple arithmetic. A few concepts from this broad section of math include:

- **Rounding and estimation:** Rarely will you need to calculate difficult numbers. Instead, you are expected to round numbers. For instance, if you end up with a calculation of 11.6^2 on a particular problem, you would choose an answer choice that is slightly less than 144 (12^2) rather than trying to multiply this awkward number. This can save you a lot of time. Similarly, when comparing numbers, you can often do so by estimating which is most likely to fit a certain scenario, rather than calculating. You may also need to estimate the square root of some common prime numbers.

- **Scientific notation:** You will need to recognize scientific notation, which is widely used on the test. For example, the number 12,000,000 might be expressed as 1.2×10^7. To find the right exponent for the 10, count the number of times you would have to move the decimal point to the left to go from 12,000,000 to 1.2. Because you would move the decimal seven places, you would express 1.2×10^7. For decimals less than 1, the exponent will be negative. For instance, 0.0034 could be expressed as 3.4×10^{-3}. Remember that the negative results when you move the decimal in the opposite direction.

- **Unit analysis:** You need to know both metric and SI (International System of Units) units and conversions for a variety of measurements, including joules (J) for energy, watt (W) for power (W = 1 J per second), amperes (A) for electric current, ohms (Ω) for electrical resistance, and pascals (Pa) for pressure.

Algebra

It stands to reason that with all of the equations you will need for the MCAT, you must also have a strong understanding of how to solve algebraic equations. In most cases, this will involve plugging in numbers for several variables and solving for another variable.

- **Proportions:** One way to avoid calculation when solving algebraic equations is through recognizing proportional variables in an equation. For instance, in the equation for kinetic energy (Ek = $^3/_2$RT), kinetic energy (E_k) is proportional to temperature (T). Therefore, if the temperature were doubled, you could simply double the figure for kinetic energy to derive an answer with very little calculation. Other variables in an equation will be inversely proportional. In the equation for the speed of a wave (v = $f\lambda$ or f = v/λ), frequency (f) is inversely proportional to wavelength (λ). So if the wavelength were doubled, the frequency would be cut in half.

Geometry and trigonometry

These two closely related subject areas show up largely in the physics questions, where problems dealing with the movement of objects will often involve the various angles at which these object are moving.

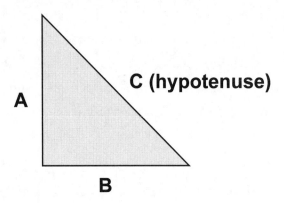

- **Sine, cosine, and tangent:** These three values can be expressed as various proportions between the sides of a right triangle. As seen in the right triangle above, the hypotenuse is the side opposite the right angle. The sine of angle BC, for instance, would be the length of the side opposite the angle divided by the hypotenuse (sin BC = A/C). Cosine would be the adjacent side over the hypotenuse (cos BC=B/C), and tangent would be opposite over adjacent (tan BC = A/B).

Statistics

Experimental questions in particular may require you to be familiar with some basic statistics terms in measurements.

- **Standard deviation:** This statistical measure tells you to what extent the numbers in a set vary from the average. You will not have to calculate standard deviation for the MCAT. However, you should recognize that a low standard deviation indicates that values in a set of data are clustered around the average, while a higher standard deviation indicates that more of the values in a set of data vary widely from the average.

- **Probability:** This is most simply expressed as the number of desired outcomes divided by the number of possible outcomes. For instance, if you have five balls in a bag and three of which are blue, the probability of picking out a blue ball at random would be 3/5, or three in five.

- **Mean, median, and mode:** The mean is simply the average of a set of numbers, while the median is the middle number when the set is expressed in chronological order. The mode is the number that occurs most frequently in a set.

- **Correlation:** Two variables are said to correlate when they tend to rise or fall together. For instance, a study of health indicators in various cities may find that cancer rates rise along with the percentage of the population that smokes. Note that a correlation does not necessarily indicate that one factor is causing the other (though in this case, it is likely). Cancer rates may just as easily rise as family income drops (an inverse correlation); this does not mean that poverty causes cancer.

Tip 59

Mastering the MCAT

Most of these math concepts should be familiar to you. If you feel you need to brush up on a few of them, bust out those old textbooks, or check out online math resources. Some of them are listed in the back of this book.

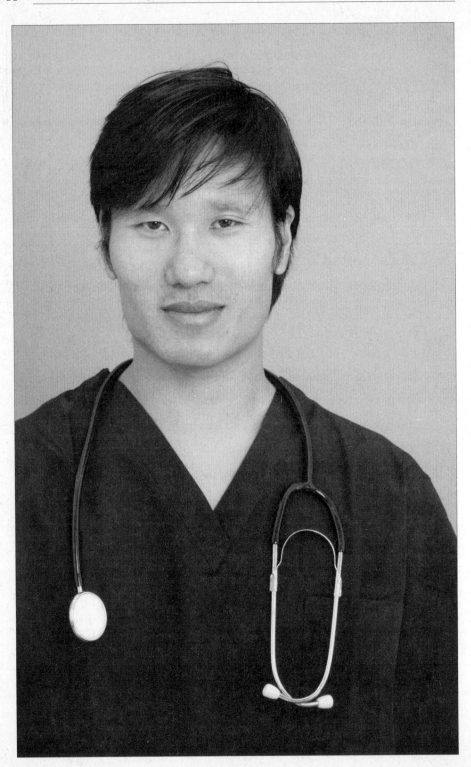

PART

02

chapter

Physical Sciences

This chapter covers what will be included in the physical sciences section of the test. The physical sciences section of the test is evenly divided between chemistry and physics, so we will play close attention to both. The "Physical Sciences" and "Biological Sciences" chapters of this book (Chapters 7 and 10) include a lot of information densely packed into their pages. The physics section, in particular, includes dozens of formulas that you should memorize by the time you take the MCAT.

Tip 60

Mastering the MCAT

As you read through this chapter for the first time, make note of which concepts are familiar and which are not. Do not be afraid to take your pen to this book. For instance, you might put checks by the concepts and formulas you remember and stars by the ones you think are most difficult.

Tackling the Physical Science Section

The previous chapter covered techniques and strategies for studying and taking the test that apply to both of the science sections. There are some strategies and techniques, however, that will be most useful in only the physical sciences section. Because physics is so heavily centered on various formulas and calculation, memorizing equations will be a larger part in studying for this chapter. While you will have to do some calculation using the formulas listed in this section, physics problems are not terribly complex mathematically; this section will not include long or involved problems that will require contortions of numbers crunching or complex use of variables or equations. The focus will be on your understanding of these concepts.

Memorizing equations

Chemistry and physics have many equations that you may find in the MCAT. An equation is somewhat different in these two disciplines, however. In chemistry, an equation is the diagram of a chemical process. Because, according to Einstein's famous conservation theory, matter and energy can be neither created nor destroyed — only converted — what you get out of any process must equal what you put in. Thus, chemical equations must always "balance" in their elements; ensuring that they do is the heart of stoichiometry. A physics equation is slightly different. In this case, it is a description in mathematical terms and symbols of a physical law or principle. Take, for example, $F = MA$: Force (in Newtons) equals mass times acceleration. So, the greater the acceleration (or the greater the mass), the greater the force exerted. This equation encapsulates a universal truth about the way objects move based different factors.

You will find the more complicated equations that are needed to answer specific questions are given to you on the MCAT, but you will be expected to know the basic ones yourself. You will not be given an equation sheet or be allowed to bring one in, so you must have these memorized. How will you know the difference? To answer that question, you will have to go back to the materials from your basic prerequisite courses. What did your professor require you to memorize? What equation sheets were you given? If you were required to memorize a formula in your early college courses, you will probably be expected to have it memorized for the MCAT. Take these and make a list of them. Break them down into different subjects, perhaps using your old syllabus or textbook to determine the organization. Obviously, this means a lot of material. How do you organize it? First, remember that you will be tested in information from freshman-level courses. Second, the time to begin studying for any major test like the MCAT is when you begin your course. Yes, that means your freshman year. When you are a premed major, you already know right from the beginning what your end goal will be: taking and doing well on the MCAT. So, why wait and shove all of that preparation into the last year of your courses?

Mastering the MCAT

When you take your freshman courses (usually the 1000-level courses), keep an equation sheet for each subject and collate these sheets at the end of your course. Put this material aside until it is time to study for the MCAT, so you will have it ready and will not need to waste time looking for those equations.

Online resources

The chemistry and physics sections of the MCAT are especially popular for online study discussion largely because they are so important. They are often the most familiar to a student who has taken many science courses. Some of these online resources are very useful; some are potentially harmful (or at least misleading); and some are neither beneficial nor harmful but probably not worth your time. Students often trade tips and changes to the latest MCAT on these boards. You can also use them as a support system of other premed majors. You can find links to online student discussion boards in the references section at the end of this book, along with other online resources that will help you immensely as you practice for the test. Keep in mind that while there are some good free resources out there, much of the MCAT information you will find on the Internet is for sale,, so some of these sites will try to sell you their book or preparation course. You may feel you need the extra push you get from a course, and you may feel that you need to purchase a book to get in-depth explanations for a subject in which you are seriously deficient. For most people, the best course of action is to create your own study plan using this book as a guide, supplementing with practice tests and other resources that you find online. Even for-profit Web sites often post some free content, such as practice tests, that you can use to get used to the test.

Mastering the MCAT

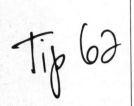

If you feel you need more practice tests than you can find for free online, your best bet would be to go directly to the source and purchase practice tests from AAMC. If you need a lot of help in a specific area, consider hiring a tutor.

However, you should take anything that you see online with a grain of salt, unless it comes directly from AAMC or a well-known source such as Princeton Review. Students, especially those who have already taken the MCAT, can give you some very good tips, and many of them do so online. This includes Wikipedia, which is a good starting point for your research but should not be relied on thorough studying. Looking up a topic on Wikipedia can point you to lots of other more reputable sources of information on that topic. Wikipedia itself, however, suffers from a few problems, both in general and for anyone studying for a test like the MCAT. The largest problem, of course, is that it can be edited by anyone. Some of the errors you may find can be quite subtle, and you might only catch them if you had already reviewed the material. You will not see such errors in your textbooks because multiple experts review them before publication. Articles in scientific journals also go through a referee process. This is not the case with a less formal resource like Wikipedia, so only use it as a tool to get to other reputable sources.

What You Need to Know About Physics
Kinematics

Concepts in the subject of kinematics include velocity, acceleration, and displacement, as well as specific, gravity-affected forms such as free fall and projectile motion. It is important to memorize all relevant formulas for this section, such as those for calculating distance, velocity, and acceleration.

Words to know

(Some terms are followed by the letters that represent them in the equations below.)

Vector	Represents the direction and magnitude with which an object moves; usually drawn as an arrow.
Speed (s)	How fast an object is moving.
Velocity (v, v_o = original velocity, v_f = final velocity)	The same as speed, but with the added component of the direction of the movement in regards to a vector over a period of time.
Acceleration (a)	The change in the rate of velocity over a period of time.
Displacement (d)	The change in position of an object from one place to another. Displacement without a vector is called distance.
Time (t)	How long it takes any of these movements to occur.
Free fall	The point in an object's fall inside a gravity well where the object achieves escape velocity (the velocity needed to escape the gravity well) and can go no faster. On earth, this escape velocity constant (ve) is: 11.2 m/s^2, while the acceleration of gravity (g) is 9.8 m/s^2.

| **Projectile motion** | The motion of a thrown projectile as it continues its motion through inertia and is being acted upon by gravity. |

Equations to know

- **Velocity:** $v = d/t$
- **Acceleration:** $a = v/t$
- **Velocity and acceleration:** $v_f = v_o + at$
- **Displacement and acceleration:** $d = v_o(t) + \frac{1}{2}(a)(t^2)$

Forces

The MCAT will deal with forces in a Newtonian system, especially those having to do with translational equilibrium (equal and opposing forces that cancel each other out). It will also deal with friction, pulleys, fulcrums, and inclined planes. You will need to memorize the relevant formulas for calculating force and friction, listed below, as well as the translation of forces along pulleys or planes.

Words to know

(Some terms are followed by the letters that represent them in the equations below.)

Newtonian	The system of physics used before Einstein introduced his theory of relativity. Newtonian physics has not been disproved. It is now considered to apply to the physics of objects at relatively low velocities (such as what we would experience in life) where relativistic distortion is negligible.
Force (F)	Something that pushes or pulls something else, either putting the object into motion or stopping it.
Mass (m)	A number, related to weight, that expresses an object's resistance to a change in motion. Weight is the acceleration of the mass due to gravity.

Friction (F_f)	When two objects are pressed together in such a way as to impede their movement when a force is applied to one or both of them.
Pulley	A wheel or other circular device that changes the force vector of a rope to allow an object to be lifted or lowered more easily by transmitting the motion.
Fulcrum	The balance point for a lever.
Inclined plane	A plane that is tilted so as to allow objects to be pushed or rolled down with the aid of gravity.
Centripetal force (F_c)	The force of an object going in a circle. The object is constantly trying to go off in a straight line due to inertia (the tendency of an object to remain at rest or continue on the same vector on which it was started by a force), but because it is held to a circular path, it goes in a circle. The centripetal force occurs due to the constantly changing vectors of the object's velocity and force.
Centripetal acceleration (a_c)	The rate of change of tangential velocity. Because the object is constantly changing vectors, it is also constantly in acceleration.
Torque (τ)	Can be a messy term — it has a different definition in engineering, for instance, than it does in physics. It applies to the force (F) with which an object moves on a lever arm. For the purposes of the MCAT, torque can be envisioned as a clockwise or counterclockwise twisting.
Rotational equilibrium	When the sum of all torques acting on it must be zero, meaning the clockwise and counterclockwise torques are equal.

Mastering the MCAT

The concept of centripetal force is also erroneously known as "centrifugal force." This is an erroneous term because it assumes that the force is pushing the object outward when, in fact, the inertia of the object pushes it at right angles to the force pulling it toward the center.

Equations to know

- **Force:** $F = ma$

- **Friction:** $F_f = \mu F$ (The μ represents one of the two coefficients of friction: one for kinetic friction and the other for static friction)

- **Centripetal acceleration:** $ac = v^2/r$ (In this and the next equation, r represents the radius of the circle created by a circular motion)

- **Centripetal force:** $F_c = (mv^2)/r$

- **Torque:** $\tau = rL$, where r is the length of the lever arm vector

- **Rotational equilibrium:** Sum of torque $= 0$

Different forms of energy

Energy questions may deal with the different forms that energy can take — namely, work, power, and momentum, as well as potential and kinetic energy, especially the transfer of energy that occurs in collisions.

Words to know

(Some terms are followed by the letters that represent them in the equations below.)

Work (W)	The transfer of energy another using force. The only other way to transfer energy is heat (Q). Work is measured in joules.
Power (P)	The rater of work; measured in watts (which, like work, are often represented by the letter W).
Energy (E)	The ability to do work. In the absence of heat transfer, the two terms are interchangeable and use the same units — joules.
Momentum (p)	The tendency of an object to stay on its current path; related to mass and velocity.
Potential energy (PE or U)	A type of energy that is dependent on position. There are two major types of potential energy on the MCAT: gravitational (energy produced by gravity) and elastic (energy produced by an object such as a spring).
Kinetic energy (KE)	The type of energy that applies to an object in motion.

Collision	The moment when two bodies meet, causing some change in one or both.

Mastering the MCAT

There are two types of collisions: elastic, in which energy is conserved because none is spent on internal energy; and inelastic, in which momentum is conserved but energy is not.

Equations to know

- **Work:** $W = F(d)\cos\Theta$ (where F is force, d is displacement, and Θ is the angle between F and d); when the force and motion are in the same direction, then $W = Fd$
- **Law of thermodynamics:** $\Delta E = W + Q$
- **Power:** $P = W/t$ or $P = \Delta E/t$
- **Kinetic energy:** $E_k = \frac{1}{2}(m)(v^2)$
- **Momentum:** $p = mv$

States

Questions on this topic will deal with at least one of the three main states: solids, liquids, and gasses. A major concept will include buoyancy, and you will see some overlap with equilibrium of forces theory. Two major equations that you will need to know will be Hooke's law and the Bernoulli effect.

Words to know

(Some terms are followed by the letters that represent them in the equations below.)

Solid	When molecules are in a fixed arrangement. This is the coldest of the states. The most important formula for this state is modulus of elasticity.

Liquid	When molecules are in a fluid arrangement and the matter can change shape, but the molecules are close enough together that they are held down by gravity. This is the medium of the states in terms of temperature.
Gas	When molecules are in a very fluid arrangement and can be separated from each other quite widely to the point of being relatively free of gravity. This is the highest temperature of these three states. A gas is considered a fluid for the purposes of the equations below.
Density (ρ)	The heaviness of a liquid or solid, in terms of its volume (V) and mass (m).
Buoyancy	The quality of how high a mass rides in a liquid and how well the liquid can support the mass.
Ideal fluid	There is no actual "ideal fluid." Instead, it is an idea that makes fluid problems less complicated by working with a fluid that has no viscosity and is incompressible. Bernoulli's equation, below, applies to an ideal fluid.
Stress	The pressure exerted on an object.
Strain	How an object is changed, or deformed, by that pressure.
Hooke's law	Measures the elasticity of a spring where the extension of a spring when it is pulled out (or pushed in) is directly proportional to the load (the force on the spring) to the point where the load exceeds the limit of elasticity.

Equations to know

- **Density:** $\rho = m/v$

- **Modulus of elasticity:** stress/strain = a constant until you reach the elastic limit, the point at which the objects are permanently deformed

- **Hooke's law:** $F = -k(x)$ where F is the force that the spring exerts in restoring its original shape, x is the distance between the spring's natural length and the length to which it has been stretched or compressed, and k is a spring constant measured in Newtons per meter

- **Bernoulli's equation:** $P_s + \frac{1}{2}(\rho)(v^2) + \rho gh = P_t$, where P_s is static pressure, P_t is total pressure, v is velocity, and h is height

Electrostatics, electricity, and magnetism

Electrostatics involves the somewhat different concepts of electricity and magnetism. Consider the former to be about electromagnetic fields at rest and the latter about electromagnetic fields in motion. Electrostatics questions may cover concepts such as electric charges and fields. Questions on electricity and magnetism may include basic electronic concepts such as voltage, ampage, currents, resistors, and capacitors of the DC variety.

Words to know

(Some terms are followed by the letters that represent them in the equations below.)

Electricity	A current generated by the interaction between an electrical and a magnetic field.
Magnetism	The phenomena by which materials attract or repulse other materials. A magnetic field has north and south poles; opposite poles attract, while like poles repulse one another.
Electric charge (Q)	Given in coulombs; a charge is the difficult-to-define embodiment of electricity. An electric charge is either positive or negative.
Current (I)	A moving charge; expressed in amps.
AC/DC	DC is direct current where the movement of electrons is in one direction; AC is alternating current in which the electrons change direction in a simple pattern.
Resistor	Anything that impedes the flow of current.
Capacitor	Anything that aids in the flow of current.
Voltage (V)	An electric field's potential to move a charge from one point to another. It is expressed by the strength of the current (I) taking into account resistance (R).
Kirchhoff's rules	Two key rules that apply to circuits. The current going into a node equals the current coming out, and the voltage around any path in a circuit will add up to zero.

Mastering the MCAT

You will most likely be tested on DC, not AC current, on the MCAT, and the equations listed here apply to DC.

Equations to know

- **Force (F) of a charge (Q) moving through a magnetic field (B):** $F = QVB\sin\Theta$, where Θ is the angle between the magnetic field and the velocity of the charge
- **Voltage (Ohm's law):** $V = IR$

Waves, optics, and sound

These three topics are all closely related, as light and sound both travel in waves. General questions on waves and oscillation could include any of the basic concepts of waves, simple harmonic motion such as springs and pendulums, and conservation of energy and momentum. As you can see, there will be some overlap with other areas such as forces, circular motion, forms of energy, and electrostatics. Optics questions will deal with the behavior of light, the fundamental optics concept — including the reflection, refraction, and light — and electromagnetic radiation. You should also know the basic concepts of optics as related to mirrors and lenses, both concave and convex.

Words to know

(Some terms are followed by the letters that represent them in the equations below.)

Mechanical wave	One of the three types of waves (also including electromagnetic and matter), this type of wave must travel through matter. These waves can be further broken down into two categories: transverse and longitudinal.

Transverse	A wave that oscillates horizontally. Light is a transverse wave, as is electromagnetic radiation.
Longitudinal	A wave that oscillates in line with the wave's direction. Sound and pressure are both longitudinal waves.
Wavelength (λ)	The distance in which a wave's shape repeats itself, usually measured between troughs or crests in a wave.
Frequency (f)	How often a wave pattern occurs.
Oscillation	A displacement from equilibrium that changes periodically over time and repeats at regular intervals, such as the swing of a pendulum.
Constructive	When two or more waves share the same length and frequency and their sines and cosines are the same, reinforcing each other. This is constructive interference.
Destructive	When two or more waves have sines and cosines that are opposite to each other, they cancel each other out, resulting in the "destruction" of the wave. This is destructive interference.
Light	Electromagnetic radiation within the visible spectrum.
Electromagnetic radiation	Wave-particles of light that vary according to length and frequency.
Reflection	When light bounces off of a surface at another angle.
Refraction	When light goes through a transparent solid, liquid, or gas and is bent. The index of refraction (n) below compares the speed of light in a medium (v) to the speed of light in a vacuum (c).
Mirror	A reflective surface.
Lens	A solid, liquid, or gas that either concentrates or scatters the light that passes through it. A lens is said to have a power (P) that is distinct from the power seen in mechanics and is related to the focal length (f).
Concave	A mirror or lens that is hollowed. This concentrates the light waves onto a smaller surface.
Harmonic motion	Any regularly repeating motion. The MCAT will most likely test the simple harmonic motion, which follows a perfect sine wave.
Convex	A mirror or lens that bulges out. This scatters the light onto a larger surface.

Doppler effect	When an object generating sound waves approaches or retreats from a listener. As the object approaches, sound waves go up in frequency as the waves are shortened (due to the shortened distance). As the object retreats, sound waves go down in frequency as the waves are lengthened (due to the increased distance).
Logarithmic scale for sound intensity level	The scale that determines the intensity of sound frequencies as measured in sound.

Mastering the MCAT

Slower, less intense radiation has a lower frequency and longer waves; faster, more intense radiation is high frequency with short wave lengths.

Equations to know

- **Speed of a wave:** $v = (f)(\lambda)$
- **Power of a lens:** $P = 1/f$
- **Index of refraction:** $n = c/v$

Stoichiometry

The fields of physics and chemistry are related to each other, so you will not always see questions that deal with these concepts in isolation. Both fields also use balanced equations, which make up a large portion of stoichiometry. It is the mathematical way, applying basic algebra, and writing and balancing equations. All chemical equations must begin and end with the all of the matter and energy involved accounted for.

For example, the reaction for the formation of water looks like this: $2H_2 + O_2 = 2H_2O$.

Here, two H_2 molecules (a molecule consisting of two hydrogen atoms) combine with one oxygen molecule (a molecule consisting of two oxygen atoms) to for two water molecules. The same number of atoms is represented on the left-hand side as on the right-hand side. Ensuring that the numbers are the same is called balancing an equation.

What You Need to Know About General Chemistry

Chemistry shows up on the MCAT in two places. General, or inorganic, chemistry is part of the physical sciences section, and organic chemistry is part of the biological sciences section.

Mastering the MCAT

While some prospective test takers may find it helpful to study the two types of chemistry together, in most cases it will likely be easier to study them as distinct parts, so that you are better prepared for the format of the test, in which general chemistry will be mixed in with physics instead of organic chemistry.

In either case, we have listed below in detail what you need to know about the chemistry concepts that you are most likely to see on the physical sciences section of the MCAT — from atomic structure to thermodynamics — including formulas and key terms.

The good news when studying for inorganic chemistry questions is that there are far fewer formulas to memorize in order to ace these questions than there are for the physics section. Instead, you will be expected to internalize the following concepts well enough so you can apply them to new situations and in concert with other concepts. As far as your approach to chemistry-based questions in the physical sciences section, you will find that it will be similar to that of the physics questions.

Mastering the MCAT

If you are much stronger in one topic than you are in the other — if the next session has you in a cold sweat, for instance — feel free to skip over the more difficult questions and return to them later. As always, you will need to put a "placeholder" answer in case you do not get back through the section, and you will need to mark which problems you skipped.

Atomic structure

Questions in this section may cover the basic concepts and properties of atomic and subatomic structures: protons, neutrons, and electrons, both physical and chemical. All of these can be found in a review of nuclear chemistry, as well as quantum numbers and electron configurations. You should also review the basics of radioactivity and radioactive decay.

Words to know

(Some terms are followed by the letters that represent them in the equations below.)

Atomic	Anything that has to do with the atom or that deals with the entire atom.
Subatomic	Anything that has to do with the particles that make up an atom or the inner workings of the atom.
Proton	A positively charged particle found in the nucleus (central mass) of an atom. It affects both the atomic weight and the atomic number (the electrical charge) of the atom.
Neutron	A particle with no charge found in the nucleus of an atom. It affects atomic weight but not atomic number. Different radioisotopes of an atom may have a differing number of neutrons.

Electron	A negatively charged particle that circles the nucleus of the atom in an electron shell that represents an energy state.
Quantum number	The atom's atomic number, or the number of protons, that define an element. The periodic table lists elements in order of their atomic numbers.
Electron configuration	The configuration of the electrons in the various shells or states.
Isotopes	Have the same number of protons but different numbers of neutrons.
Radioactivity	The tendency of some unstable (radioactive) atoms to emit particles such as protons, neutrons, and electrons until they reach a more stable energy state.
Radioactive decay	The process by which atoms change from one element to another by emitting particles. This process can range from less than a second to thousands of years.
Mole	A unit of measurement for the mass of an atom based on the number of carbon atoms in 12 grams of Carbon-12; also known as Avogadro's number.

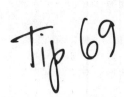

Mastering the MCAT

It is important to note how the movement of electrons can change the overall charge of an atom. For instance, an electrical charge will cause an electron to jump "up" a shell further away from the nucleus. Lack of charge will allow an electron to drop down a shell. This is why an excited atom can become ionized (achieve a positive or negative charge): It can lose its electron, causing it to achieve a more positive charge.

Equations to know

- **Atomic number:** Number of protons
- **Atomic weight or mass:** Number of protons and neutrons
- **Moles:** Grams/atomic or molecular weight

Periodic trends and bonding

Questions in this section are related to those of atomic structure, but involve molecular and atomic bonds. You will need to review the physical and chemical properties that affect melting and boiling points and viscosity, as well as vapor pressure. There will also be some overlap with organic chemistry in molecular geometry involving covalent bonding and ionic bonding.

Words to know

(Some terms are followed by the letters that represent them in the equations below.)

Atomic bond	Occurs within an atom; binds protons and neutron together inside the nucleus and binds the electrons to the nucleus. This bond is quite strong.
Molecular or covalent bond	Occurs between atoms and involves the sharing of one or more electrons between the atoms. This bond is weaker than an ionic bond.
Ionic bonding	Where one atom loses an electron to another, which results in both having a charge: positive for the atom that lost the electron and negative for the one that gained the electron.
Physical property	Affects the physical state of an element or compound but does not change it at the molecular or atomic level. For example, melting ice or boiling water does not change the chemical nature of water. It remains water.
Chemical property	Affects the chemical state of an element or compound in a way that changes it into another element or compound by breaking the atomic or molecular bonds or forming new ones. For example, running an electrical current through water breaks it up into two elemental gasses: hydrogen and oxygen. In a chemical reaction, then, the molecular structure of an element or compound will change.
Balanced equations	When a chemical reaction is represented as an equation, the same elements in the same number must appear on both the left and the right. Take the following example: $SnO_2 + H_2 \rightarrow Sn + H_2O$. This is not balanced because there are two oxygen atoms on the left side and one on the right. To balance this, you would add a two in front of "H_2O" on the right and another two in front of "H_2" on the left, creating this balanced equation: $SnO_2 + 2H_2 \rightarrow Sn + 2H_2O$.

Theoretical yield	The amount of product that should be left after a reaction is completed. However, many reactions stop before they are completed. Comparing the theoretical and actual yields of a reaction results in the percent yield, as listed below.

Mastering the MCAT

The opposite charges in an ionic bond draw the two atoms together like two opposing magnets, creating a bond that is stronger than the covalent bond and requiring far more energy to break.

Equations to know

- **Percent yield:** (Actual yield/Theoretical yield) x 100

Phases

As in physics, phases involve the different states of matter: solids, liquids, and gasses. You should be aware that changes between phases occur only when energy is exerted in the form of work or heat. You will also need to know how to plot graphs for pressure versus temperature and temperature versus heat, which the formulas below will help you do.

Words to know

(Some terms are followed by the letters that represent them in the equations below.)

Pressure (P)	The force exerted over an area, including an area occupied by a gas. For instance, the atmosphere exerts pressure on the earth.
Heat (Q)	A way of releasing energy. The amount of heat energy in a given substance will decrease as the surrounding temperature decreases.

Heat capacity (C)	Measures how much energy it would take, mainly in the form of heat (Q) to change the temperature (T) of a substance. Specific heat capacity is the heat capacity per unit of mass.
Phase diagram	Provides a visual representation of the phases of a given substance at different temperatures and pressures.
Colligative properties	Depend on the number of solute particles, not the type particles. The four colligative properties are vapor pressure, boiling point, freezing point, and osmotic pressure.
Melting point	The temperature at which an element or compound transitions from a solid to a liquid. The molecular bonds are loosened due to the energy of activation.
Boiling point	The temperature at which an element or compound transitions from a liquid to a gas.

Mastering the MCAT

To understand colligative properties, consider collagen, a protein in egg whites. Collagen turns into a solid when heated but does not turn back to a liquid than cooled.

Equations to know

- **Heat capacity:** $C = Q/\Delta T$
- **Phase change:** $Q = mC\Delta T$, where m is the mass of the element or compound changing phase, c is the specific heat of the element or compound, and ΔT is the change in temperature

Solutions, acids, and bases

Questions in this area all involve solutions of chemicals in water or other liquids. You will need to know about solubility, concentration, and the properties of collagens. Acid-base chemistry involves the concept of pH and what level it falls on the range of acid to base.

Words to know

(Some terms are followed by the letters that represent them in the equations below.)

Solution	The suspension of a solid or liquid (solute) in a liquid (solvent) without the two combining chemically.
Vapor pressure	The pressure exerted by a vapor on a solid or liquid phase of the same substance when they are at equilibrium.
Solubility	The ability of a solid or liquid to let another be dissolved into it.
Concentration	The number of atoms of a solute dissolved in a liquid. It is how much solid has been, or can be, dissolved in a liquid. There are several ways to measure concentration, including molarity (M) and molality (m).
pH	pH measures the level of free hydrogen ions, with a range between 1 and 14 (7 being neutral, having no reaction one way or the other).
Acid	Has a higher concentration of free hydrogen ions than a neutral element or compound. On the pH scale, anything lower than 7 is an acid; 1 is the strongest, with the highest concentration of hydrogen ions (giving it a high negative charge).
Base	Has a lower concentration of free hydrogen ions and a higher concentration of OH ions. On the pH scale, anything higher than 7 is a base; 14 is the strongest, with the lowest concentration of hydrogen ions and the highest concentration of OH ions.
Salts	Neutral ionic compounds that create acids or bases when dissolved in water.
Buffer	Any element or compound that neutralizes an acid or base by reducing the number of ions, hydrogen, or OH, pushing the acid or base to 7.

Equations to know

- **Concentration units:** M = moles of solute/volume of solution; m = moles of solute/kilograms of solvent
- **pH** = $-\log[\text{H}+]$, in which the brackets indicate concentration

Kinetics

In this area you must know how variables affect a kinetic reaction (not to be confused with kinematics), specifically the variables of temperature, rate, concentration, and catalysis. Catalysts are compounds that speed up or slow down the rate of a reaction. You should also study rate laws and rate constants. One thing to keep in mind when it comes to kinetics is how this subject differs from the physics concept of thermodynamics. A catalyst, for example, does not change the rate of a reaction by changing the laws of thermodynamics; it changes it by lowering the energy of activation.

Words to know

(Some terms are followed by the letters that represent them in the equations below.)

Mastering the MCAT

The most important aspect of rate law on the MCAT concerns forward rate, or the rate of an initial chemical reaction.

Kinetic molecular theory	A theoretic model of an ideal gas created to mitigate the complexity of gases in the ideal gas law. The ideal gas has no volume, has perfectly elastic collisions, and exerts no forces. Its average kinetic energy is proportional to its temperature.
Partial pressure	The amount of pressure exerted by any one gas to the overall pressure from the mixed gas. Dalton's law says that the partial pressures of each gas in a gaseous mixture add up to the total pressure exerted by the mixed gas.
Effusion	Where gas spreads from high pressure to low pressure through a small opening known as a pinhole.
Diffusion	The other type of gaseous spreading where a gas spreads into empty space or another gas.

Real gas	The volume of a real gas will be greater than the ideal gas because the molecules in a real gas are closer together. Also, real gases will exert less pressure than an ideal gas would.
Kinetic reaction	Kinetics is centered on how quickly a kinetic reaction occurs as it nears equilibrium. The MCAT is unlikely to ask specific questions that require computation of kinetic reactions.
Activation energy	The energy threshold at which colliding molecules may create new molecules from a kinetic reaction.
Rate law	A formula by which one can calculate the rate, measured in molarity per second, of a given kinetic reaction as it approaches equilibrium. This rate is related to temperature, pressure, and concentration of the substances involved.
Rate constant (k)	A number proportional to the reaction rate that represents the speed of a chemical reaction.
Elementary reaction	A reaction that occurs in a single step.
Catalysis	The process by which an element or compound is used to affect the rate of a chemical reaction, either to (usually) speed it up or to slow it down. Catalysis occurs frequently in biological processes to regulate them in a way that supports life.
Equilibrium	The balancing of reactions and equations detailing those reactions. Because chemical reactions are reversible, chemical equilibrium is reached when the forward and reverse reactions are equal.

Mastering the MCAT

In addition to its application in kinetics, the term "equilibrium" also has applications in thermodynamics, electrochemistry, acid base chemistry, solubility, and reaction yield.

Equations to know

- **Ideal gas law:** $pV = nRT$, where n is the number of moles of gas and R is the universal gas constant

- **Average kinetic energy:** $E_k = {}^3/_2 RT$

- **Forward rate:** Rate $= K[A]^m[B]^n$, where A and B are the reactants and m and n are the orders of each reactant

- **Equilibrium constant:** $K = \text{Products}^{\text{coefficients}} / \text{Reactants}^{\text{coefficients}}$

Thermodynamics and thermochemistry

For questions regarding thermochemistry and the chemistry-based applications of thermodynamics, you will need to know the general laws of these disciplines as well as the laws of entropy and enthalpy. You will also need to be able to define a system and its surroundings.

Words to know

(Some terms are followed by the letters that represent them in the equations below.)

Thermodynamics	The study of energy, as noted in the section on physics. In chemistry, thermodynamics is most concerned with the relationship between energy and complex chemical systems. Chemistry-based thermodynamic functions are based on probabilities and are broken into two parts: the system and its surroundings.
System	The body being studied in a thermodynamic function. Isolated systems do not exchange energy or mass with their surroundings. Closed systems share only mass, and open systems share mass and energy.
Surroundings	Everything else in the universe other than the system.
Thermochemistry	The study of energy transfer during chemical reactions.
Entropy (S)	The tendency of all reactions and operations in the universe to eventually run out of energy and run down, losing cohesiveness and coherency as they go.

Enthalpy (H)	The heat content of a reaction; it is a man-made construct meant to explain why the capacity of a system to do work varies from its internal energy (U).
Gibbs free energy (G)	The non-PV energy available in a particular system to do work.
Equilibrium	When you get a balance of chemical operations, as evidenced by a balanced equation in stoichiometry.

Equations to know

- **Work:** $W = P\Delta V$
- **Entropy:** $\Delta S = Q/T$
- **Enthalpy:** $H = E + pV$
- **Gibbs free energy:** $G(p, T) = H - TS$

Electrochemistry

Electrochemistry is a branch of chemistry that deals with how electricity acts in chemical reactions and how it is produced by chemical reactions. Questions from this area deal with the concepts of oxidation, reduction, and other aspects of an electrochemical cell. You should also know the difference between a galvanic and an electrolytic cell.

Words to know

(Some terms are followed by the letters that represent them in the equations below.)

Oxidation-reduction reaction (redox reaction)	A reaction in which electrons move from one atom to another.
Oxidation	The process of losing an electron during a reaction. The atom that loses an electron in a redox reaction is considered oxidized.
Reduction	The process of gaining an electron during a reaction. The atom that gains the electron in a redox reaction is considered reduced.

Oxidation states	The various forms an atom will take as it undergoes a redox reaction.
Galvanic (or voltaic) cell	A type of cell that changes chemical energy from a redox reaction into electrical energy that can be used for work.
Electrolytic cell	A cell that uses electricity from an external source to create a redox reaction.
Electrochemical cell	A more general term that can refer to either galvanic or electrolytic cells.
Anode	A terminal on a battery that has a negative charge.
Cathode	A terminal on a battery that has a positive charge.

Physical Sciences Practice Exercises

1. If a motorboat travels 5 knots per hour west for three hours, but the wind pushes it back at 3 knots per hour, how far does the boat go?

   A. 5 knots.
   B. 6 knots.
   C. 3 knots.
   D. 0 knots.

2. Electricity is created by placing zinc and copper solutions in two half-cells connected by a salt bridge. Which of the following is NOT true?

   A. The electricity is produced by a galvanic cell.
   B. The electricity is produced by a voltaic cell.
   C. The electrical energy is produced by the movement of electrons.
   D. The salt bridge is used to draw extraneous molecules from the reaction, creating a greater electrical output.

3. A child is riding on an amusement park ride. She sits in a seat that swings around a central pole on a chain. Which of the following would represent how fast she is moving?

    A. The square root of [(the force pulling her toward the center pole times the distance from her to the pole)/the combined mass of the girl and her swing].

    B. (The force pulling her away from the center pole/the force pulling her toward the center pole) times the combined mass of the girl and her swing.

    C. The square root of [(the force pulling her away from the center pole times the distance from her to the pole)/the combined mass of the girl and her swing].

    D. The square root of (the force pulling her toward the center pole/the mass of the girl and her swing).

4. Which of the following is true of the sound waves emitted by a racecar as it approaches the point on the track closest to your seat at the racetrack?

    I.   *Their frequency, as observed by you, is higher than the frequency of the waves emitted by the car.*

    II. *Their wavelength, as observed by you, is higher than the wavelength emitted by the car.*

    III. *They make the sound you hear higher-pitched than the sound the car is actually making.*

    IV. *They would make the sound you hear higher-pitched than it would otherwise be only if you were walking toward the track.*

    A. I and III only.

B. I and IV only.

C. I, II, and III only.

D. I, II, and IV only.

5. **The partial pressure of atmospheric oxygen gas at sea level is 160 mm Hg. If the oxygen makes up 21 percent of all atmospheric gases, which of the following is NOT true of hydrogen, which makes up 78 percent of the atmosphere?**

A. Its partial pressure is roughly 600 mm Hg.

B. The pressure exerted by hydrogen is greater than the pressure exerted by an ideal gas.

C. Ozone makes up less than 1 percent of atmospheric gases.

D. The pressure exerted by the atmosphere is greater than 700 mm Hg.

6. **A man jumps off a bridge with a bungee attached to his foot, and his head just touches the water before he bounces back up. Which of the following statements is true?**

A. The greater the elasticity of the bungee, the greater the force pulling the man toward the water.

B. The longer the bungee, the greater the force pushing the man back toward the bridge.

C. The greater the difference between the normal length and its length when the man hits the water, the greater the force pushing the man back toward the bridge.

D. Hooke's law will apply once the bungee has reached the elastic limit.

chapter | *08*

Verbal Reasoning

The verbal reasoning section tests general-reasoning and critical-thinking skills derived from the humanities. The section aims to assess your ability to quickly determine the main point and important facts of a passage by asking you to answer questions about the passage based on that knowledge. The verbal reasoning section is intimidating to many students because there is a good deal of material to read that must be analyzed quickly to answer questions based on that analysis. All of this must be accomplished within a single hour.

You will have 60 minutes to answer 40 questions based on seven passages, each approximately 600 words long. This will give you five to seven questions per passage. The most intimidating and potentially time-consuming part of this section is usually the reading. Reading under a deadline can seem like a daunting task, particularly if you are a slow reader. Some passages require more time than others to absorb, even if they are the same length, and which ones you will need more time on can be difficult to predict. If you are put off by the idea of that much ink on paper, try putting the task in perspective: A passage of 600 words in a standard font such as Times New Roman can fit neatly onto one page single-spaced. This means that you are only required to read seven pages of passages in the entire reading section. Of course, you must also answer 40 related questions, all within an hour.

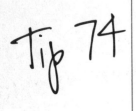

Mastering the MCAT

If you put aside 20 minutes total to read the passages, this leaves you 40 minutes to answer the questions, which translates to nearly three minutes to read each passage and one minute to answer each question. While this is a tight schedule, it is not an impossible goal to meet. The three minutes per passage are for your initial reading, which need not be exhaustive because you will most likely need to glance over the passage again once you read the questions.

You have some tools that can aid you in the verbal reasoning section, including the highlighting function of your computerized test, scratch paper, and your knowledge of how to locate and analyze the main idea of the passage. You can also make notes on the paper where you found important information. This will help you keep track of the significant information, particularly the main idea. It is important to keep in mind as you complete the verbal reasoning section that the reading is only part of it. You also have to analyze what you read and then answer the questions. Remember: Do not spend *all* of your time reading.

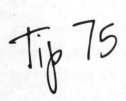

Mastering the MCAT

With the highlighting button, you can mark the main idea and any pertinent information that appears so you can use it when you start to answer the questions. This is an important time-saving device. You do not want to search and search again for the same information.

The Passages

Familiarize yourself with the types of writing you are likely to encounter. Some will argue that you should practice reading before you take the test, while others will say this is a waste of time. In reality, how you practice reading will dictate how effective that practice is.

Mastering the MCAT

If you practice reading to further your skills in analyzing and answering questions about your reading, then it will help you. If you simply read, that will not help you much. It may teach you how to read faster, and perhaps improve your vocabulary in a general way, but in order to see any real improvement, it is necessary to practice analyzing the text.

The short, nonfiction passages you see on the MCAT can be roughly sorted into three categories: articles, essays, and scientific papers. One of the biggest differences between the types of writing is where they put the main idea and how it is presented. Though you are taught in school to write a three- or five-paragraph essay where the main idea and thesis statement appear in the introduction, this does not mean that all essays, let alone all articles, follow this pattern. Do not expect to see this pattern in the passages in your verbal reasoning section, as the types of writing used on the MCAT vary widely in their structure. In the verbal reasoning section of the MCAT, you will see a few different types of passages.

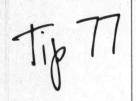

Mastering the MCAT

Some essays introduce the main idea immediately. Others introduce it further along in the passage, and still others toward the end of the essay. Some never state the main idea outright at all, and you have to come at it yourself from what you see in the passage. Therefore, be aware that a major part of your analysis will involve determining where and what the main idea is based on what type of nonfiction the passage is.

Newspaper articles

In a newspaper article, the main idea and most important information will appear in the headline and first four paragraphs. The most common newspaper article structure, known as the inverted pyramid style, puts the most important information first, with the rest of the information in descending order of importance. That way, a reader who is pressed for time can get the most important facts even if he or she does not read the entire article. When updating a running story, journalists will simply add the new information to the first few paragraphs, along with the most important information, and move the older or less relevant information further down. This ensures that anyone reading the new version of the article need merely read the first four paragraphs to be brought up to date. Newspaper articles have other common attributes, including:

- Dry, objective language (just the facts)
- May use language like "proof" and "evidence"
- Authoritative tone
- Balanced view that does not take sides

Once you have identified a passage as a newspaper article, you should be leery of any answer choices with strong language or ones that imply the author is expressing a strong point of view on the issue. In this largely objective type of writing, this type of language is invariably present only in the wrong answers.

Essays

Essays can be a bit tricky because each essay writer may have a slightly different purpose for writing, and they can vary widely in structure in tone. When reading essays, pay close attention to what the author is trying to do. Is he hoping to convince readers of a particular point of view, or to spur action of some time? Many questions will focus in some way on the overall point of the work. Is he critiquing a particular idea, or proposing a new one? Also pay attention to the author's tone, as the correct answer choice will mimic that tone, whether it is somber, straightforward, or impassioned.

Argumentative essays

An argumentative essay has a very strong thesis — often one that the writer anticipates some readers will disagree with, or one that itself expresses disagreement with a previous idea or theory. The author therefore presents his or her main idea, thesis, and main arguments early in the essay. The rest of the essay involves proving the thesis and usually includes a counterargument that some readers may initially agree with, but the author therefore disproves. Argumentative essays appear on topics where there are strong opposing positions, such as global warming or abortion, thus making strong theses possible. Some attributes of these essays include:

- Strong, sometimes harsh language
- May use language like "proof" or "evidence"
- Authoritative tone
- Controversial

Argumentative essays lend themselves to questions about structure, as in which examples are used to support what idea. As you are reading these essays (and others, as much as possible), pay attention to how the author supports his or her main assertion using specific examples. Jot down a few notes on what is in each paragraph and which examples seem most important. Some of these will likely show up in the questions.

Persuasive essays

Persuasive essays can be seen as a gentler form of the argumentative essay. Here, the author does not automatically assume that the audience is hostile to his or her thesis. Therefore, the thesis is less forcefully presented, and the emphasis is on persuading the audience to the author's point. In persuasive essays, the main idea and thesis can be articulated quite late — even at the end of the essay in some cases — particularly if they are controversial. Persuasive essays often embody the following attributes:

- Less forcefully stated tone than the argumentative essay
- Evidence used to support the author's thesis

Because these are less forcefully stated than argumentative essays, identifying the overall purpose and main idea can be a bit more difficult, particularly when you are dealing with only a portion of the entire essay as it was written. Look for a single statement that seems to encapsulate the overall idea of the essay, and jot it down on scratch paper in your own words. Keep in mind it could just as easily be at the end as the beginning.

Comparison essays

A comparison essay compares two or more things. Usually, this involves two similarities and one difference, much as the argumentative essay involves two arguments and one counterargument. A contrast essay compares items that are more different than they are similar. In this type of essay, you see more differences than similarities between the things being compared.

- Tone varies depending on essay type (argumentative or persuasive)
- Uses language that compares and contrasts two or more things
- Common comparison words: such as, like, as, in addition
- Common contrast words: despite, although, however, but, in contrast
- Stronger tone in contrast than in comparison essays
- Comparative language that emphasizes differences

Comparison essays are all about what is the same and what is different about the various ideas presented. The key to answering these questions, then, is often keeping straight which is which. This can be more difficult then it sounds when the essays are dense with complex language. To keep everything straight in your mind, try jotting down notes in two columns, one labeled "compare" with attributes shared by the various components being discussed, and one labeled "contrast" with the attributes that differ.

Descriptive essays

In a descriptive essay, the thesis in this essay is usually so weak and nebulous that writing instructors despair at seeing it, even if many students enjoy this type of writing, in which they can enjoy some creative liberties. Some instructors may even tell you that a descriptive essay has no thesis, but this is not true. All proper, nonfiction writing has a thesis, whether it is clearly stated, implied in the context of the passage, subtly hinted at, or even poorly stated. Some signs of a descriptive essay are:

- Subjective, vivid language
- Authoritative tone

You may well see these passages on the verbal reasoning section precisely because the thesis (and even the main idea) can be so difficult to identify and analyze. This makes for a good test of critical thinking skills. These are also good for questions on the use of language, so jot down notes on any words or phrases that are repeated frequently in the passage or stand out to you as conveying an important idea. The more often a word is repeated, the more important it is to the overall main idea of the passage.

How-to essays

How-to essays are a type of descriptive essay where the author explains to the audience how to do something. The main idea or thesis in this type of essay is usually straightforward, even if it can sometimes be hard to find. The main idea is what the audience is being instructed to do, and the thesis is how the audience can do it.

- Objective language
- Authoritative tone
- Noncontroversial (assumes audience already agrees with thesis)

The devil is in the details in this type of essay, which is rarely seen on the MCAT. Questions on these types of essays might focus on details within the process being described that are so miniscule, it is difficult to parse them out. Be sure to go back to the passage to look for each answer in the text.

Scientific papers

A scientific paper presents an experiment or the problem an experiment is set up to test, reviews related literature, describes the experiment, and discusses the results. Types of this writing can include the write-up of an experiment or theory in a journal. The main idea is the subject of the experiment or problem, and the thesis is the hypothesis or theory to explain why the subject occurs.

- Objective language
- May use language like proof and evidence
- Authoritative tone
- May be controversial

Scientific papers are largely about method, so you can ask yourself similar questions as you would on the science sections of the test. Does this experiment seem valid? What holes can you find in the logic of the experiment? What kind of other study might be required to bolster this theory? Expect the questions to focus in on these critiques of the experiment or theory.

Mastering the MCAT

You need to learn how to recognize these different types of writing because you could see any of them in the verbal reasoning section. Each type affects the structure, how the main idea is presented, and where it appears in the essay. If you can recognize these types of writing, you can identify the main idea in them that much more quickly and readily, thus saving you a lot of time on this section.

Reading and Analyzing the Passages

Chances are, you knew how to read long before you took organic chemistry. Still, the prospect of wading through unfamiliar texts and answering tricky questions about them can be just as daunting as the biology section for many test takers. The following tips will help you get the most out of the passages, which is the first step in choosing the right answer.

Writing style

The respective writing types vary more than just in the presentation of their main idea. There are also differences in style, voice, argument, and presentation of evidence. Some essays use anecdotal evidence. Others use only statistical facts and analysis. Some use a warm, persuasive tone that may hide arguments and the main idea or thesis. Others have a strong, even harsh or strident, voice. Many of the questions on the MCAT will require you to understand how the author's style, tone, and structure contribute to his or her argument, or even why he or she may have chosen to use such devices.

One aspect of writing style to pay close attention to is the tone, which is basically the writer's voice. Tone can mask things that the writer is trying to say or things that the writer does not want the reader to see. For example, if the writer believes that the audience will be hostile toward a point, he or she will downplay the aspect of that point because it could alienate the audience. The writer may also feel unable to address a counterargument that an audience may find particularly persuasive. A writer who puts forth a certain argument is generally expected to address the counterargument and show the audience why it is not persuasive or why it actually supports the writer's thesis. However, some writers may mask the counterargument and distract the audience away from it. The writer can do this in several ways:

- Flatter the audience or set up a straw man argument — an argument so ridiculous that no one would genuinely hold it
- Attack opponents at a personal level (ad hominem argument) or in other ways that have nothing to do with the main idea or thesis
- Use strong or emotive language to mask a weak or false argument

For example, Adolf Hitler is reviled as one of the worst mass murderers in history, but he was able to persuade many otherwise normal and compassionate Germans to his cause. Hitler had a highly persuasive oratorical style, enhanced all the more by well-studied rhetorical flourishes when he spoke, which conveyed a sense of group unity in crowd settings and gave the listener a lofty feeling of being part of a greater purpose and higher ideals. As detailed in Leni Riefenstahl's documentary *Triumph of the Will*, Hitler did not begin with the more odious or hostile aspects of his message — racism and genocide. Instead, he began by reinforcing group identity and solidarity in his listeners, by flattering them and making them feel part of a "master race." Only then, once he had drawn them into his verbal spell, did he introduce the darker and more controversial aspects of his message.

This is a more common technique than you might think. The writer will often try to appeal to emotion rather than logic. This might occur by appealing to and reinforcing positive self-esteem, as Hitler did. Or a writer might take the opposite approach, deliberately setting out to upset, offend, or even anger the reader. This can be just as effective in hiding things the writer does not want you to see as positive appeals.

Mastering the MCAT

Pay close attention to the author's tone, and do not let yourself be carried away by a writer's faulty logic, as the questions for such a piece will almost certainly test your assessment of it. Do not expect all the passages that you read to be in a clinical or objective tone.

This holds especially true for humor, such as satire, that sets out deliberately to offend you in order to get you to think about a part of the author's message. Jonathan Swift's essay from 1729's *A Modest Proposal* is a classic example. It is a satirical suggestion to the poor Irish of the early 18th century to fatten up Irish babies in order to sell them as meat, like pork or beef, to an English market. Being Anglo-Irish himself (an English gentleman born and raised in Ireland), Swift felt that indifference in the British Empire to the plight of the Irish had contributed to chronic poverty in Ireland. He felt his English audience would likely not respond well to an emotional appeal, so he chose to take the opposite tactic and shock them with a literal, extremely outrageous straw man argument. Swift knew that British cultural sensibilities would recoil at such a bald restatement of the situation as an attempt to profit on the backs of the Irish, not by exporting food while people were starving (which was already occurring), but by overt infanticide and cannibalism. Swift used this horrific example to expose the hypocrisy and civilized indifference that had led to the problem in the first place.

The first three paragraphs of Jonathan Swift's *A Modest Proposal*

It is a melancholy object to those, who walk through this great town, or travel in the country, when they see the streets, the roads and cabin-doors crowded with beggars of the female sex, followed by three, four, or six children, all in rags, and importuning every passenger for an alms.

These mothers, instead of being able to work for their honest livelihood, are forced to employ all their time in strolling to beg sustenance for their helpless infants who, as they grow up, either turn thieves for want of work, or leave their dear native country, to fight for the Pretender in Spain, or sell themselves to the Barbadoes [sic].

I think it is agreed by all parties, that this prodigious number of children in the arms, or on the backs, or at the heels of their mothers, and frequently of their fathers, is in the present deplorable state of the kingdom, a very great additional grievance; and therefore whoever could find out a fair, cheap and easy method of making these children sound and useful members of the common-wealth, would deserve so well of the public, as to have his statue set up for a preserver of the nation.

But my intention is very far from being confined to provide only for the children of professed beggars: it is of a much greater extent, and shall

> take in the whole number of infants at a certain age, who are born of parents in effect as little able to support them, as those who demand our charity in the streets.

Look carefully at what Swift is doing in the above paragraph: He is creating a word picture. He is presenting an image of the Irish poor for his audience, the British, who are hostile toward the Irish. The Irish are not merely poor; they are destitute. They are not merely destitute; they are homeless beggars and thieves. They are petty criminals (mercenaries). They have an alarming number of children. They are sick. They are dirty. You may notice that Swift makes them sound like human vermin by using words and phrases like "crowded" and "prodigious number" and giving an image of the children "on the backs, or at the heels of their mothers," much in the way that fleas, ticks, or rats might cling.

The main purpose of the first two paragraphs is to get the audience to trust Swift. He is playing to their racism and class prejudice, largely subconscious and denied. This is to draw in the audience and prepare them for what Swift is about to do. In one way, he is getting their sympathy, but in another way he is drawing them into a trap. In the third paragraph, he begins to close the trap — he tells his audience that he has a modest proposal that will help "provide" for these many children. Here Swift appeals to the audience's affection for small children, but at the same time raises their fears of being overwhelmed by the higher numbers of Irish offspring. What he is doing is gradually dehumanizing these children so that his audience will accept his "proposal."

Unfortunately for Swift, while his essay did get his message across to more people than a straight appeal might have, it also gained him a terrible reputation. Readers who could not understand what he was trying to do took his words at face value and called him a monster for advocating the killing of babies. If you took that approach and analysis on the MCAT, you would not come out well because you would not be able to differentiate between a straightforward factual proposal and a clearly satirical work; this could lead to many missed problems.

Abridged works

As we discuss how to read and analyze an abridged work, let us continue considering *A Modest Proposal*. Swift's original essay was nearly 3,400 words long. However, if it were to appear on the MCAT, you will see only an excerpt of about 600 words. Nearly all MCAT passages are abridged forms of larger works (such as long articles or books). This adds to the unusual structure of some of these passages, as they will be parts of a complete work rather than one with a coherent beginning, middle, and end. The fact that you are not reading a complete work should in turn influence how you approach them as you read.

For example, if you saw an excerpt from *A Modest Proposal* on the test, you might see only the first fifth of the essay — or worse yet, the third fifth of the essay, which would contain even less introductory material. You might be initially confused by the main idea because you may be missing an introduction. To help yourself gain some frame of reference for abridged passages, keep the following questions in mind as you read:

- Who might have written this text?
- Why?
- Are there references that seem to refer to part of the text that is missing?
- What can I guess about the text from them?

Find the main idea

Even if everything else is a blur, you need to have a good grasp of the main idea to answer the verbal reasoning questions correctly. Though only two or three of the questions may be directly about the main idea, everything in the essay relates to it. Otherwise, the author would not put in that material. Everything describes, supports, appears to refute, or reiterates the main idea, so it will crop up in many different forms.

In most essays or articles, you will find the main idea in the first few paragraphs. In the standard five-paragraph or three-paragraph essay you wrote in high school, the main idea was introduced in the first paragraph. Not all types of nonfiction do this, but they usually introduce the main idea (or at least some clues) within the first three paragraphs. Readers are impatient, so the writer must hook them in sooner rather than later. In some of the more difficult passages, however, the main idea is buried. In Swift's text, for example, only after a long and rambling passage in which he explains why the children of poor Irish people cannot be supported in good health does Swift state his "modest proposal":

> I have been assured by a very knowing American of my acquaintance in London, that a young healthy child well nursed, is, at a year old, a most delicious nourishing and wholesome food, whether stewed, roasted, baked, or boiled; and I make no doubt that it will equally serve in a fricasie, or a ragoust.

Nine paragraphs and 815 words in, he gives us both the main idea and thesis of his essay — that the Irish are starving because they have produced too many children, and the solution is institutionalized infanticide and cannibalism.

Sometimes, the main idea is never stated outright, but you can understand it through the rest of the context. This means that while you could not quote the main idea as any phrase or sentence from the passage, you could *infer* it by circumstantial evidence that you found in the passage or information that you know about the author or passage. For example, by knowing that Jonathan Swift was a satirist who bitterly opposed the British social policies in Ireland, you could infer that his essay was satirical and that his real main idea was the opposite of what it appeared to be in his essay.

Another way to hone a difficult-to-find main idea is to look for word patterns. You should note any repeatedly used vocabulary words, facts, or figures on your scrap sheet for future reference. Repetition indicates importance in an essay. What is the word that continually comes up in Swift's essay? Children; variations of child or children are in every paragraph. Swift also constantly discusses the problem that there are too many poor Irish children but subtly hints that the reason why there are "too many" children is that they are starving due to their parents being unable to find work. He also supports the idea that the Irish have more children than they can afford when he mentions that his proposal would not only solve the problem of the overpopulation children but also eliminate the use of abortion and infanticide to regulate the number of children. Therefore, Swift is hinting that Irish mothers are not having more children than they can feed because they want to or are lazy, but because they have no other options. He further hints that his fellow English countrymen and women hypocritically deny the Irish any means to solve their plight themselves, then turn around and blame them for being unable to solve it. These word, phrase, and theme repetitions therefore reiterate and expand upon his true main idea and thesis.

Finding arguments

Once you have isolated the main idea, you will want to keep track of the arguments the author is using to support the main idea. In general, you should be paying the most attention to verbs and subject nouns, which can guide you to the meaning of a text even if it is fogged up with clauses and other distractions. You should especially look for subject nouns and verbs in the topic sentence of each paragraph of the passage in order to locate the author's various arguments.

The topic sentence in a well-constructed paragraph is the first sentence. It introduces the topic of the paragraph. If you are in a hurry — starting the last passage with only a few minutes left, for instance — you can scan the passage by reading the first three paragraphs, the topic sentences of other body paragraphs, and the concluding paragraph. Ideally, you will keep better track of your time so that you can take in more nuanced information as you read. For example, look at the first sentence of this paragraph taken from the middle of a sample passage:

> The Devil has been presented in many forms through the ages. In Greek and Roman times, he was not evil, but a legitimate god, king of the underworld, called "Hades" or "Pluto." In the Old Testament, Satan was an angel of the Lord. In Christian times, he began to be presented as evil in nature. The afterlife of the pagans was divided into Heaven and Hell. Satan, who had been cast out of Heaven, was in charge of Hell. Initially, he was presented as a beautiful, but sinister, angel, but as the centuries passed, his appearance became more and more grotesque. He went from seducing sinners to evil to terrifying them from doing it. Ironically, his later appearance in Christianity went back to being more like his initial appearance as a grim, terrifying figure.

As you can see, this passage has many details, but they all tie back to the topic sentence: "The Devil has been presented in many forms through the ages." There is also an argument (that the Devil took on at least two distinct types of forms) that structures the examples, but the main point is in the paragraph's first sentence. Notice the repeated nouns and verbs (devil, hell, pagan, presented) reiterate this overall idea throughout this short passage.

Mastering the MCAT

As you read the passages the first time, you do not want to focus on the details; you can go back to find the details when a particular question requires you to do so. Instead, you want to focus on these general arguments so that you create a mental map of where the supporting details in the text will be found.

Highlighting

Highlighting is a very useful tool in the verbal reasoning section. With your mouse, you can click on key words and phrases in a passage and highlight them for future reference. This can be quite helpful, but overuse of it can confuse you instead of helping you. Also, keep in mind that this highlighting will disappear once you move to another passage, so should you go back to an earlier passage, you will no longer see your highlighting.

Mastering the MCAT

When highlighting, it is tempting to highlight entire sentences, lines, even paragraphs. Resist this urge. When you highlight a section in this way, it indicates that you have not thought sufficiently about why this section of the passage needs to be remembered for whatever reason.

If you take the extra moment to determine what is important to highlight and why it is important to distinguish it from the other text, you will find your highlighting far more efficient. Here are some tips to help you improve your highlighting technique:

- Highlight no more than one line

- Highlight a single word or short phrase that you absolutely need

- Try not to highlight more than once in one paragraph

- Pick the word or phrase that will connect you to the parts that you want to remember

- Mark down what you highlight on your scratch paper to help you remember them

- Highlight important words, such as transition, cause and effect, or emphasis words

Here is an example of some words you might have highlighted in the sample passage we have been discussing:

The Devil has been presented in many forms through the ages. In Greek and Roman times, he was not evil, but a legitimate god, king of the underworld, called "Hades" or "Pluto." In the Old Testament, Satan was an angel of the Lord. In Christian times, he began to be presented as evil in nature. The afterlife of the pagans was divided into Heaven and

Hell. Satan, who had been cast out of Heaven, was in charge of Hell. Initially, he was presented as a beautiful, but sinister, angel, but as the centuries passed, his appearance became more and more grotesque. He went from seducing sinners to evil to terrifying them from doing it. Ironically, his later appearance in Christianity went back to being more like his initial appearance as a grim, terrifying figure.

In this case, the highlighting served to keep track of the various changes in the devil's appearance and presentation discussed in the passage by highlighting nouns and verbs that describe him in chronological order.

Another way to help you remember information from the passage is by making an annotation. Write down the topic of a paragraph in three words or less to use as a quick reference when you reach the questions. Annotations can be useful when you note the main idea of the passage and the topic of each paragraph. You can write down specific words or phrases. For example, let us return to the paragraph about the Devil. A three-word description of this paragraph could be: *Devil many forms*. You do not need to make it a complete sentence, but just enough to get the general idea. Once you have noted the main idea and topic sentences on scratch paper, you can use them as a reference for the questions that you will answer.

What to Look for in Questions

Questions in the verbal reasoning section come in sets based on a reading passage. The question order is not random. For example, the first one or two questions are usually about the main idea and will involve testing your ability to identify and discuss it. Subsequent questions may be about organization or voice. Strictly factual questions are fairly unusual. In the verbal reasoning section, you will see the questions begin at a general, fundamental level, then proceed to more specific questions about the details, approach, intent, or tone. You may be asked to determine when the passage was written and find the ultimate intent of the author. As in other areas of the MCAT, you should choose the most comprehensive answer, not just one that is correct for part of the question. When answering a question, try following these steps:

- Analyze the passage
- Read the question
- Read the answers
- Eliminate wrong answers

- Choose the correct answer, or guess between the remaining choices if you are unsure
- Reevaluate the final answer to make sure that it answers the question

Question format

There are generally three formats of questions in the verbal reasoning section of the MCAT. The MCAT exists to test your skills and, in the case of the verbal reasoning section, your skills in reading comprehension and analysis. Therefore, the questions will not be overly creative.

Multiple choice

Most of the questions you see will be in the standard multiple-choice format. In multiple-choice questions, the tester asks a question and you are given four possible answers. The following sample question and explanation will show you how to use the steps above to find the correct answer:

▶ **Judging from the first three paragraphs of** *A Modest Proposal,* **the problem Jonathan Swift hopes to remedy with his proposal could be:**

  A. The proliferation of beggars in Ireland.
  B. The slave trade in Barbados.
  C. The starvation of children in Ireland.
  D. Extreme worldwide poverty.

As with many MCAT verbal reasoning questions, you see here that it is fairly easy to eliminate some answers, while at least two seem to be correct. You should be able to eliminate answer choice (**B**) quite quickly because Barbados is mentioned only in passing as a possible destination for Ireland's poverty-stricken youth. You may be tempted by answer choice (**A**) because beggars are mentioned in several paragraphs. However, in the last paragraph he makes it clear that he is hoping to help the children of beggars (and others), not the beggars themselves. As if often the case, then, you are left with two choices, both focused on the children in question. One answer choice, however, is too broad. You might not know enough about Swift to realize that he is writing about Ireland; the country's name is not mentioned. However, he does specifically say that the problem he is discussing occurs in this country or kingdom. Therefore, answer choice **(D)** is incorrect because it is too broad. The passage talks about the necessity of supporting the children of the poor Irish, so the answer is **(C)**. Even if you did not know that the passage was about Ireland, the "could be" phrasing of the question allows Ireland to be the correct answer.

Negation

The previous question was phrased in a straightforward way, as in "which one of these is correct?" Some of the questions in the verbal reasoning section will approach their topics backward by asking which of the answer choices is *not* correct. This is called negation format, and it occurs when you get a statement that excludes one or more options, usually with the words "not" or "except" in capital letters. Take, for example, this practice question based on the sample paragraph from earlier in this chapter:

▶ **Which of the following is NOT a form taken by the Devil mentioned in the text?**

A. An attractive but malevolent being.

B. A horned god.

C. An angel.

D. A king.

Negation questions take advantage of a weird quirk in the way the mind works that makes you want to choose the answer you have seen, even if you are asked to choose the one you have not seen. The key to answering them is to use the process of elimination. You can do this using your memory at first, but you will likely have to refer to the text, also. In this case, two of the answer choices are easy to find: **(C)** and **(D)** are both clearly mentioned in the text. From there, you may not recognize the phrasing from answer choice **(A)**, and you may remember from your own experience that the devil has been represented as **(B)** a horned god. Once you review the text, however, you will see that there is no mention of this representation. On the other hand, the phrase "an attractive but malevolent being" is similar in meaning to "a beautiful, but sinister, angel." Because "horned god" or some equivalent does show up in the text, the answer is **(B)**.

Roman numerals

Another type of question asks you to choose from among several statements marked with Roman numerals. These questions can be tricky because they are really asking you to choose multiple true or false answers. The main thing to concern yourself with in this type of question is that you pick the answer that has all of the true conditions in it, not just some of them. Because this requires an extra level of evaluation, this type of question can eat a lot of your available time. Be cautious about getting too wrapped up in one of these questions. Try this one, based on the paragraph above:

▶ **Which of these statements is true?**

I. *Satan is an angel.*
II. *The Devil is the lord of Hell.*
III. *Hades is a demon.*
IV. *Hades and Pluto are names for similar Greek and Roman gods.*

A. I only.

    B. I and II only.

    C. I, II, and IV only.

    D. III and IV only.

To answer these questions, you should check each statement separately. The passage states that Satan is an angel **(I)** and also the lord of Hell **(II)**. There is no mention, however, of Hades being a demon **(III)**. It further states that Hades and Pluto are similar characters who rule the underworld in Greek and Roman beliefs. **(IV)**. However, it also tells us that Hades is a god and does not mention demons at all. You might know that demons and gods are not the same thing already, but you do not need to know the difference for this passage. It already gives you all the information that you need. No external knowledge of the subject is required. The answer is **(C)**.

Question types

Within these three different formats, the verbal reasoning questions will test different reading comprehension skills. Therefore, your approach to the questions should also vary by their type. Here are some of the types of questions you will encounter, along with some tips for how to approach different questions. As you do practice sets, try to identify these question types and use the strategies below to answer them.

Main idea

These questions ask you about the main idea of a passage. In a way, all questions in the verbal reasoning section ask you to answer questions about the main idea. However, main idea questions ask these directly and involve the meaning or intent of the main idea, rather than how it is presented or supported or inferred. When looking at a main idea question, always remember that such questions are about the entire passage, not a part of it. When evaluating whether a question is about the main idea, look for emphasis words and phrases like main point, main idea, main purpose, or central theme. You may get less forthright questions that begin with things like "the author believes that..." This is just another way of asking you about the author's point of view, which is usually the main idea of the passage.

The two best ways to determine a main idea question are finding the emphasis words and determining the scope of the question. Look for main idea questions toward the beginning of question sets, as questions in a set tend to move from general to specific. Look for an answer that covers the passage generally rather than a specific section, paragraph, or sentence. The answer to a main idea question that is only true for one section of the passage cannot be the answer because the main idea must hold true for the entire passage. When reading through the passage, look for the subject, the idea that governs the entire passage. This usually appears within the first three paragraphs.

Retrieval

Retrieval questions involve the retrieval of information that is clearly stated in the passage. It will usually be an important statement but may be a detail that is fairly difficult to find. A retrieval question is a bit like an archeological dig in which you are trying to find something that is there in the passage but may not be obvious at first glance. Because this is such a general and common type of question, you can analyze it under the assumption that it is a retrieval question. This is where your notes come in handy. If you annotated the paragraphs, simply look at your notes and look for a paragraph that has the right subject for the question. Now that you have narrowed the field, look through the paragraph for a correct answer and then see if it is in your answer set.

Look for key words (important nouns or verbs in the passage that also appear in the questions or answers) or proper names in the questions, such as those of people or places in the passage. You can also look for words of emphasis (such as "important" or "necessary"), or cause and effect (such as "because" or "therefore"). Watch out for answers that look good or correct only because they are in the passage, though; these are false positives. The answer should not just be locatable in the passage; it should also be the correct answer to the question. You should watch out for answers that talk about details that are not important in the passage or that appear to be a quote from the passage, yet twist the meaning around.

Inference

Inference questions ask you to answer a question that uses information from the passage, but not in a literal way. As such, the answers to inference questions will not be direct quotes, but more paraphrases of quotes from the passage. The use of the word "infer" should clue you in that you are getting an inference question, as well as words and phrases like "imply," "most likely," "suggest," or "reasonable to conclude."

Inference questions on the MCAT do not require you to make large steps from the evidence in the passage. Choose the answer that answers the question in a way that is closest to the passage — one that paraphrases the information and retains the tone of the passage. As always, the inference being made in this question is likely to be related to — and will definitely be consistent with — the overall main idea of the passage.

Inference questions are tricky because they ask you to step outside of the passage and make an inference from it that is not exactly stated. However, you are still limited to the information in the passage. Watch out for words or phrases that express too strong or extreme a statement, or that discuss information you would not find in the passage.

Mastering the MCAT

Always remember that the main point of the verbal reasoning section is to test your ability to analyze and answer questions about a passage. Resist the urge to bring your own education to the table in the verbal reasoning passage. That is not what you are being asked to do. Do not use information that is not already in the passage; instead, extract and use that information from the passage to answer the question.

Application

Application questions ask you to take the information from the passage and apply it to a new situation proposed in the question. You are essentially using the passage as a resource to answer the question rather than a basis for the question. Application questions are related to inference questions in that they do not ask you a question where the answer can be found literally in the passage. An application question usually employs speculative verbs such as "imagine" or "suppose" and phrases such as "this information, if true." "If" is one indicator of an application question.

As with inference questions, the danger is in getting too far away from the passage and not answering the question, or picking an answer that is not supported by the passage. A good rule of thumb with application questions is to avoid using information that is not in the passage or the question. The passage has the basic information with which you can answer the question. Any information about the new situation that you must consider is introduced in the question. Avoid thinking outside of these two boxes. Furthermore, an application question is usually about the main idea in some way. So, when faced with such a question, the first thing you should do is determine the main idea and then figure out what the question asks about it. If the question is about a specific part of the passage rather than the main idea, it will usually signal that by directing you to a specific part of the passage or a specific idea that is only mentioned in part of the passage.

Strengthen/weaken

These questions ask you to determine the strength or weakness of the author's main idea or thesis. They use the words "strengthen" and "weaken" but also may use words such as "support," "bolster," "challenge," "attack," or "undermine." These questions are evaluation questions. Rather than identify or discuss the main idea as the main idea, you are being asked to evaluate its strengths and weaknesses. It can be easy to mix up the two, so try marking down which one is which before answering the question. Try going through a passage and marking down the various arguments. Then, label them as ones that strengthen, weaken, or do not apply to the author's main idea or thesis.

Unlike other question types, where you want to avoid language that is too strong or absolute, here you need to look for it. Avoid weak or equivocal wording like "may/might," "some," "sometimes," or "occasionally." Here are examples of the types of strengthen/weaken questions you might see on the MCAT:

- How do the quotes from Shakespeare's letters strengthen the author's argument that he really did write his plays?

- Does the contradictory information found in the diary weaken the author's claim that the novelist used her own experiences in her stories?

- Why does the account of the siege of Stalingrad bolster the author's thesis that the Russians suffered the most in WWII of the allied powers?

- How does the last paragraph challenge the author's claims in the previous paragraphs?

- Does the exclusion of the villain from the discussion of the novel attack the author's theory about the villain's weakness in the story?

- How does the use of quotations out of context ultimately undermine the author's points?

Look for strong statements that prove the author's claim the way it needs to be to fulfill the task of the question. If you are looking for a statement that strengthens the claim, look for a strong and unequivocal one. If you are looking for a statement that weakens the claim, look for one that disproves it outright. Do not go for a partial victory or compromise here.

Support

Support questions ask you to evaluate a word or phrase and how well it supports the author's argument — this is usually, but not always, the author's main idea. They will often have the word "support" in them. The passages used for these questions are not easily understood or analyzed, so avoid any answer that is too straightforward. If the answer were that straightforward, there would be no reason to ask a question about it. When answering the question, remember that it is a quote, and look at the context by reading the sentences around it. Often, the answer to the question is a paraphrase of a sentence in proximity to the quote.

Hybrid

Retrieval and inference questions are frequently mixed together. They both involve retrieval of information. Strengthen/weaken questions can also be mixed with application questions because both ask that you apply your knowledge of the passage to the question. On these questions, stick to the text for your answers, and avoid answers that stray too far from the text or that are not directly supported by it. They are unlikely to be the correct answers. Look for the support, mark it down, and compare it to the answers. The one with the most textual support is probably the correct answer.

With these questions, you may need to take more time than usual. Combining two difficult types of questions like the strengthen/weaken and application types usually increases the difficulty. If you find yourself flummoxed, make an educated guess and move on. These questions are relatively few, so you do not need to worry.

Strategies for answering questions

You should be practicing strategies for answering MCAT questions well before the test. Learning how to deal with the MCAT in the middle of the test is likely the worst mistake about the test you could make outside of not studying properly. Here are some suggestions for strategies to get used to using as you practice for the verbal reasoning section.

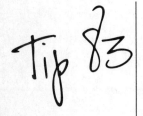

Mastering the MCAT

Remember that the MCAT is a test of scientific skills, even in the verbal reasoning section. As such, approach any answers that sound vague, emotional, hostile, or otherwise unscientific (not rigorous and objective) with extreme caution. If it sounds unscientific, it is not likely to be your answer.

1. Avoid absolute language

The verbal reasoning section of the MCAT tests your analytical skills; this means that you are using the skills of the scientific method to find the answer. Theories exist to be modified to accommodate new information, not as an absolute to be followed without discussion or opposition. Therefore, absolute or extreme wording is unlikely to be found in the right answer for a verbal reasoning section because statements using such broad language often make broad assumptions that cannot be supported by evidence. Absolute language includes words such as "all," "every," "never," "only," "always," and "none." Extreme language would include emotion-laden words such as "offensive," "vulgar," "derogatory," "evil," "beautiful," "wonderful," or "great" in reference to the passage. Some examples of absolute language that you could see on the MCAT — and that is likely to indicate a wrong answer choice — include:

- All animals used in experiments suffer terribly.
- Everyone knows that global warming is a fact.
- We will never know how the dinosaurs died.
- Only people who can sing well can truly appreciate music.
- There are always those who are willing to spoil a good thing.
- None of the weather forecasters who predict weather are any good at it.
- This passage makes offensive statements about Native Americans.
- The vulgar tone of this passage detracts from the author's thesis.
- The author makes derogatory comments about his enemies that discredit him.
- The evil that this passage advocates cannot be overemphasized.
- The beautiful language in this passage enhances the thesis.
- The author uses many wonderful metaphors to support her main idea.
- This is a great passage because it explains clearly why animals should be protected against exploitation.

You may notice that another commonality in both absolute and extreme language is their imprecision. This kind of language appeals to your emotions, not your logic. Stay objective. Another sign that an answer choice is likely to be wrong is imprecision in expressions of time. Phrases such as "since the beginning of time," "for many years/centuries/millennia," or "years ago" are imprecise. Look for passages that match any timetable that appears in the passage. Avoid imprecise expressions of time, especially if they do not appear in the passage itself.

2. Stay within the parameters of the passage

Just as you should avoid imprecision of time, you should also avoid taking too many liberties with the text of the passage. Even in inference questions, you want to avoid going too far outside of the parameters of the passage, and especially the question. Focus on answering the question; avoid reading too far into it.

3. Be suspicious of big words

Another thing to watch out for in the MCAT is the use of overly convoluted terminology — or, put simply, big words. Answers with big word answers can trip you up by sounding authoritative. You may tell yourself that the answer sounds like the right answer — perhaps it sounds like just the way your teachers would say it. You may be intimidated by the words because you are not sure what they mean but do not want to admit that. Big words are not enough. They must also be the *right* words.

4. Eliminate choices with relationships that do not exist

Relationship answers can be tricky because inference and application questions both ask you to make these kinds of connections. When looking at a relationship answer, keep in mind that the relationship should exist in the passage; that it should be as the passage indicates; and that it should be relevant to the question.

5. Do not settle for partial answers

These are answers that answer part of the question but not all of it. These are tricky because on the MCAT, you will be in a hurry and may not see that only part of the question is being answered. This is why it is so critical that you know the question well enough to be able to determine when you have found the answer to it.

Mastering the MCAT

You can help yourself in the verbal reasoning section by remembering your main task: answering the question. If the option that you pick does not answer the question, however elegant it sounds, it is not the correct answer.

Sample Questions and Explanations

The following questions, and the explanations that follow them, exemplify some of the wrong answer types and other strategies mentioned above. Pay close attention to the process of elimination used in these examples, and try to use that process yourself as you complete the exercises that follow these examples. Look again at the passage about the Devil, and these sample questions based on it:

> The Devil has been presented in many forms through the ages. In Greek and Roman times, he was not evil, but a legitimate god, king of the underworld, called "Hades" or "Pluto." In the Old Testament, Satan was an angel of the Lord. In Christian times, he began to be presented as evil in nature. The afterlife of the pagans was divided into Heaven and Hell. Satan, who had been cast out of Heaven, was in charge of Hell. Initially, he was presented as a beautiful, but sinister, angel, but as the centuries passed, his appearance became more and more grotesque.

> He went from seducing sinners to evil to terrifying them from doing it. Ironically, his later appearance in Christianity went back to being more like his initial appearance as a grim, terrifying figure.

1. **The author most likely discusses the evolution of the Devil's appearance through the ages for which reason?**

    A. European women were often accused of witchcraft during the 16th and 17th centuries due to the Devil's reputation as a seducer.

    B. Through the ages, the Devil has always been presented as a sinister figure.

    C. The image of the Devil, though it has changed considerably between Old Testament and Greco-Roman times and the later Christian period, appears to have essentially come full circle because both the Greco-Roman Hades and the later Christian Satan are intended to be terrifying.

    D. The alterations in the pictorial imagery of the personification of evil in Greco-Roman and Christian times were mutated by the sociopolitical upheavals during these historical periods.

This statement in answer choice (**A**) could be argued to be true in general because one of the accusations against witches during the witch crazes was that they had sexual relations with the Devil as part of their pact with him. However, this information falls outside the parameters of the question. The question asks why the author of the passage discusses the evolution of the Devil's appearance; the author never mentions witches or witchcraft. Also, the question asks the reader to find a general statement about the entire time period cited by the author. Despite the vague time indicator at the beginning ("through the ages"), the author does give a specific time period and place that includes Europe in Greek and Roman times up to the later Christian period. This answer, while getting the area specified in the passage (Europe) right, has too narrow a temporal focus to answer the question fully.

In the opposite direction, answer choice (**B**) is also incorrect. Though the passage uses the term "through the ages," it also gives a more precise time frame for its comparison of the Devil's images. Using the term as the only indicator of time period in the answer, therefore, makes the answer imprecise. The answer also includes extreme language. It states that "the Devil has always been presented as a *sinister* figure" — yet the word "sinister" does appear in the passage. The passage only uses this word to describe the Devil's appearance in one of the periods described. Therefore, the answer is inaccurate. Do not assume that just because a phrase or quote in an answer also appeared in a passage, the answer must be correct. A correct answer must do more than quote pieces of a passage to be correct.

Answer choice (**D**) may have also been tempting. How, you may ask, can such a smart answer be wrong? It does not answer the question, though; it just obscures the fact in fancy language and big words. The author never mentions pictorial images of the Devil. The author could also be talking about literature. Nor does the author mention a "personification of evil" because he or she is discussing a specific character in mythology: the Devil. There are many different characters in Greek, Roman, and Christian mythology that are evil (personifications of evil), but this passage only discusses one of them. Nor does the author discuss social or political issues in the passage during any of the "historical periods" referred to in the question. So, the term "sociopolitical upheavals" is irrelevant to the answer.

Answer choice (**C**) is correct. First, it answers the question. Second, it uses the same time parameters as the passage. Third, it does not contradict the author's thesis or information in the passage. Fourth, it uses a key word from the text (terrifying) to show the author's intent.

2.   **Which of these statements is true regarding the figure of the Devil in the passage?**

A.   The Satan of later Christianity was the same type of figure as the Greco-Roman god from which he derived.

B.   Despite his change in nature over time from a god to a demon, the Devil's appearance in Greco-Roman mythology is similar to his appearance in later Christian times.

C.   Hades from Greek mythology is the same figure as Lucifer from Christian mythology, only with a different name.

D.   Lucifer in early Christianity is the same figure as Satan in later Christianity.

This questions focuses on the relationships between the various figures in the passage. The answer is factual, but it is easy to be confused by the tangled relationships, so take these types of questions slowly and double-check your answer in the text. Answer choice **(A)** sets up a relationship between Satan and the pagan god Hades/Pluto that does not exist. A direct relationship is implied in the passage; however, it is different from the one stated here. This answer states that the two figures were the same, but the passage actually says that they *looked* the same. The author clearly states that Hades is a god who rules the underworld, while Satan is a fallen angel or demon who rules Hell as a sort of consolation prize after being cast out of Heaven. They are not the same type of figure, so the relationship is false.

Similarly, answer **(C)** states a direct but nonexistent relationship where Hades and Lucifer are exactly the same being. However, the passage clearly states that they are two different figures. Hades was a god who ruled the underworld and was equal to other gods. Lucifer (who later evolved into Satan) was a fallen angel who was cast down to Hell by God and turned into a demon. They are not the same.

Answer **(D)** asserts that Lucifer in early Christianity is the same figure as Satan in later Christianity. While one could argue this point because Satan evolves out of Lucifer, the passage states that Satan is different in appearance and purpose from Lucifer, something that this answer does not address. Lucifer is a beautiful seducer, Satan a terrifying demon. Answer **(D)**, therefore, is not the *best* answer.

Answer **(B)** acknowledges the change in nature that answers **(A)** and **(C)** do not. It also discusses the passages statement that the Greco-Roman version of the Devil and the Devil of later Christian times are similar in appearance, which answer **(D)** does not do. Answer **(B)** is therefore both the best answer and the correct one for this question.

Verbal Reasoning Practice Exercises

Below is a practice set with an essay and questions for you to answer. The answers can be found in the back of the book. You should time yourself when reading and when answering the questions. This way, you will be able to evaluate and improve your time as you go along. Timing yourself from the beginning of your study in verbal reasoning exercises will also help you school yourself out of any ruts. Remember that you have two places where you could get stuck: the reading and the answering of questions. But you should spend about three minutes to read each passage and only about a minute on each question in order to complete the section on time. Therefore, you should plan to complete this practice set in ten minutes.

The Role of Private Enterprise in Putting Man into Space

By Thomas Sullivan

*Thomas Sullivan, the author of this article, is an IT consultant/search engine optimizer, pilot, and space enthusiast. He manages the Web site Pilot Portal USA — Pilot Weather Briefing, Flight Schools USA, Aviation Directory (**http://pilotportalusa.atspace.com**). Send questions or comments to Sullivan; his e-mail address can be found on his Web site.*

Source*: Article Geek (**www.articlegeek.com**) — Article reprinted in original format.*

Has NASA, the monolithic space agency, failed in its quest to put man out into the cosmos? Will profit coupled with man's need to explore be the driving engine which sends man into the cosmos? Think about what has moved technology forward within the American society over the past 100 years or so. Were Orville and Wilbur Wright employed by the government? Of course not. Most of their research and development for the invention of the airplane took place within a small bike shop in western Dayton, Ohio, the birth place of aviation. Thomas Edison, who is accredited with 1,093 patents, earning him the nickname "The Wizard of Menlo Park," used his own money to build the Menlo Park research labs in New Jersey. In 1889 Thomas Edison established the Edison General Electric Company. Thomas Edison is considered the most prolific inventor of our time, and his inventions were created within the realm of private enterprise. Did the seed for the invention of the personal computer germinate within a government lab? The invention of the personal computer came from an assortment of various inventions and from the tinkering of Steve Jobs and Steve Wozniak in Job's garage in an area now called Silicon Valley. Their tinkering led to the development of Apple Computers. The story of Bill Gates and the development of the Microsoft family of operating systems took place within private enterprise. The Windows family of operating systems is the most widely used on Earth and has been a major player in bringing information technology to the developed world.

Examples of major technological advancement within the realm of private enterprise are numerous. Most major technological advancements within society have occurred outside the purview of government intervention. Governments were intended to govern the people. The government's role is to preserve the environment of freedom and democracy so that intellectual curiosity can flourish within this environment. The government's role is also to provide funding, and should not be in the nuts and bolts operation of putting man into space. The ingenuity of man within the realm of private enterprise has resulted in most of the technological advancements we enjoy today.

The cosmos will be explored by man operating from the base of private enterprise, and the technology needed to explore the cosmos will be developed within that enterprise. Why is this so? NASA is an agency driven by fear of tragedy. More mishaps will decrease the probability of sufficient government funding. This cycle of fear, mishaps, and the hope for continual funding is one that seems to have no end. But mishaps are part of the business of putting explorers into space. What can better withstand the expected mishaps? A government agency or private enterprise. If a private enterprise fails, its competitor can step in to fill the gap, and the engine of private enterprise can continue to push man into space. NASA is not a private enterprise competing within the world market place.

NASA is not what it used to be during the Apollo days. Given its current mindset and culture, it will be difficult within this framework to send man out into the cosmos as true explorers. They have given the nuts and bolts of putting man into space to private contractors. But these NASA contractors have the same NASA mindset because they are under the dominion of NASA. There is a fear of mishaps within contractors without true competition within the marketplace. NASA awards contracts to the lowest bidder. Does the lowest bidder provide the highest level of safety? Once a company is awarded a contract, they remain a NASA contractor for many years and simply become an extension of NASA. Therefore, NASA becomes an autocratic agency with its arms extending outward to many companies. NASA's manned space flight program can do no more than low earth orbit. Year after year of low earth orbit does not excite the American people. Astronauts today are no longer household names. An American president here and there will give a speech saying we are going to Mars. Even President Bush's January 14, 2004-speech seems to have already been forgotten by the American public.

When we went to the moon, this was the start of an exploration. A goal was set on May 25, 1961, by President John F. Kennedy, during a speech before a Joint Session of Congress, to reach the moon before the end of the decade. NASA kicked into high gear and achieved one of the greatest accomplishments in the history of mankind. We took the first step into space and then just stopped. Since then, all the manned space missions have never gone beyond low earth orbit, and the American public becomes bored easily. To gain the American interest and support of the Apollo days, we must send true explorers out into space. NASA wants to take such small, time-consuming incremental steps that by the time comes when the really exciting work begins, the American support and interest may be eroded to the point where NASA may no longer have the financial means by which to accomplish such an endeavor. Hence, the need for private enterprise to accomplish such an endeavor. If we are going to go into the cosmos, then let's do it and stop the futile activity.

A private enterprise is not a bureaucracy. If safety issues arise from qualified personnel within a bureaucracy, these issues may not resonate to the proper people within the organization. A case in point: the knowledge of a strong potential for an O-ring failure at low temperatures between the segments for the solid rocket boosters of the space shuttle existed within the bureaucracy of NASA before the Space Shuttle Challenger explosion. More specifically, this critical information in terms of probability of O-ring compromise was expressed by engineers at Morton Thiokol, the contractor for the development and production of the solid rocket boosters. This information never percolated upward from Morton Thiokol to the proper people within the NASA organization.

In private enterprise, which is non-bureaucratic by nature, a relatively small group of people are working toward a common goal. In this situation, safety issues which arise will be known by all members of the organization. Safety issues will not get lost in a bureaucracy. NASA depends on its contractors to deliver a high level of safety. A private enterprise depends on itself to provide a high level of safety. The structure of a private enterprise is more suited to the endeavor of sending out explorers into space. The government should award grants to the most promising companies with the understanding that the sending out of explorers into space does indeed benefit mankind.

Americans are at their best when they compete. Competition is an integral component of American society. What was the driving force that put us on the moon? It was the competition with the Russians. At the present moment in time, this type of competition does not exist, although it appears as if China may be a future competitor. Americans need to compete to accomplish something. It is competition which drives the advancement of technology. Why not let companies compete for government funding and let the research and development occur within these companies, and — most importantly — let them compete? These companies can have the same characteristics of any company that wants to produce a viable product. They will not be under contract from NASA and will operate as a separate private enterprise entity. A company can make money from space tourism, and the same company can be involved in sending explorers out into space. Government grants can be awarded based on how strong the potential exists for space exploration. A company can be involved in space tourism, exploration, or can provide a research and development platform. This is the future of man's endeavor into space.

Man will be exploring the cosmos with private enterprise being the driving engine. If one enterprise fails, one of the competing enterprises will win out. Sure, there will be some disasters, and risks will be taken because that is the nature of the business. But when unfortunate disasters or mishaps do occur, the private enterprise engine will not grind to a complete halt. Burt Rutan and his Scaled Composites team have taken the first steps toward this archetypical dream of exploring the cosmos, and they did it with a fraction of the budget that NASA uses and with a team of 130 or so people to boot. They won the Ansari X-Prize by sending a man into space and returning him safely to earth, and then they repeated this within two week — an absolutely unbelievable accomplishment given the facilities and resources that were available to them. This could only occur within a society where freedom and democracy are regarded as a right to all individuals. The United States is such a society.

Burt Rutan has said that he has never worked a day in his life. He only plays. His passion for his work is what produces results. Burt Rutan and his team represent the core of what makes the United States the greatest country in the world. Maybe terrorists can get it through their thick heads that freedom does work. Most importantly, Scaled Composites has shown the world what private enterprise can accomplish. Even if Scaled Composites' endeavors never go beyond earth orbit, they have taken the first step within the proper mindset and culture, and this is what will put man into the cosmos. This mindset and culture of pure unadulterated intellectual curiosity is what really will put man into the cosmos — not NASA's mindset of fear.

NASA has played its important role by lighting the torch in sending man to the moon. We are now at a point in the history of mankind where that torch should be passed to private enterprise. The developer of the Ansari X-Prize, I'm sure, shares my thoughts. God has placed the planets and all the stars within the universe there for a reason. It is God's intention for us to move outward into the final frontier. We do this to fulfill the natural curiosity that God has given to us, and in the process we better the lot of mankind. Let's go...

1. **According to this article, what is the main reason why NASA has not gone farther into space?**

   A. The American public gets bored easily.

   B. NASA does not have enough competition.

   C. NASA is a government bureaucracy that avoids risks.

   D. There have been too many tragedies in the space program.

2. **What does the author believe we should do in the future to further the cause of space travel?**

   A. Get rid of NASA.

   B. Increase private enterprise in space travel.

   C. Get into a competition with another country.

   D. Only do big programs like the Apollo program from now on.

3. **Name one technological innovation that the author does NOT mention in the article.**

   A. The Macintosh computer.

   B. The car.

   C. The airplane.

   D. The space shuttle.

4. **According to the author, what was the main problem that caused the Challenger crash?**

   I. *A faulty O-ring.*
   II. *A lack of communication between the company and NASA.*
   III. *An overly complex bureaucracy.*
   IV. *Government interference.*

   A. Only I is correct.
   B. Only II and IV are correct.
   C. Only I, II, and IV are correct.
   D. Only I, II, and III are correct.

5. **What is author saying about Burt Rutan when he says, "Burt Rutan has said that he has never worked a day in his life."?**

   A. Burt Rutan has a poor work ethic.
   B. Burt Rutan has never held a regular job.
   C. Burt Rutan is very committed to the idea of space travel.
   D. Burt Rutan does not expect to get paid for his work.

6. **What does the author mean by the term "space tourism"?**

   A. Visits by civilians to NASA-run facilities such as the International Space Station.
   B. Trips to the moon.
   C. Visits to the Smithsonian National Air and Space Museum.
   D. Round trips in low earth orbit vehicles.

chapter 09

Writing Section

Writing the two essays can be the most intimidating part of the MCAT. Most of the people who apply to medical school are science-oriented rather than humanities-oriented, and so many of them find writing more difficult than studying organic chemistry equations or electromagnetic formulas. That said, you must still do well on this section, and that requires more than simply writing a few incoherent or indifferent paragraphs and calling them an "essay."

Writing the essay does not have to be intimidating, as long as you stay organized and remain aware of your time constraints. Due to the fact that you only have 30 minutes for each essay, this will usually limit your essay to between 500 and 800 words. As such, you are looking at the very simple essay structure of a prompt, followed by a counterargument, and then a final paragraph proving the essay prompt either true or false. As you can see, this task is not as bad as you might think.

Most reputable sources will tell you that the writing section — and the even verbal reasoning section — are not weighed as heavily as the science-based sections of the MCAT. There is truth to this assertion, particularly pertaining to the writing section, which is scored separately and on a different scale. However, many schools receive so many applications for their limited medical school slots that they are bound to use whatever tools they have at their disposal to eliminate candidates; this includes the writing score. In most cases, the writing score will be weighed against other parts of your score and overall application. A strong candidate who has stellar scores on the other sections might skate by with a lousy writing score; someone who is already on the border might be dropped from the list because of it.

Mastering the MCAT

Because there is a good chance your top medical schools will not weigh the writing section as heavily as the others, do not waste an inordinate amount of time preparing for the essays. However, you do want to complete several practice essays, at least until you are comfortable writing a coherent essay that fairly represents your writing ability within the allotted time.

Scoring the Essay

Each essay is scored on a 1–6 scale, with 1 being poor and 6 being excellent. Half-points are allowed, but not quarter-points or smaller. The aver-

J = 1.0 (poor)
K = 1.5
L = 2.0
M = 2.5
N = 3.0
O = 3.5 (average)
P = 4.0
Q = 4.5
R = 5.0
S = 5.5
T = 6.0 (excellent)

age is taken between the scores given by the two graders for each essay and then converted into a letter grade ranging between J and T. Each half-point raises you a grade.

What do graders assess? They look for the most obvious things, of course — grammar, spelling, sentence structure, and style. While graders are aware that anyone writing in a hurry will make a few sloppy mistakes, they will reduce your score for repeated mistakes or persistent mistakes that cloud the meaning of your essay. They also look for how you address the prompt, formulate your counterargument, and establish whether the prompt is true or false. These latter concerns are by far the most important. When writing the essay, always focus on what the graders will actually grade, rather than concerns that will hardly matter to them. Your essay, for example, needs to explain and support (or refute) the prompt, but it does not need to be elegant or eloquent — merely clear and reasonably persuasive.

Two graders will grade your essay on a scale of 1–6, then those two scores will be averaged to reach your score. The graders will likely spend very little time reading your essay before they assign it a score. They do not use a point-by-point system but give it an overall grade based on their general impression gained from only a few minutes. They grade a large number of essays at a time, so you will have even less time to make an impression than it took you to outline the essay, let alone write it. First impressions are not everything. An essay that starts off well but bogs down later will not do very well. Your first paragraph should include a strong and clear restatement of your prompt. Hook in your skeptical reader. Do not wait to do so even until your second paragraph — that could be too late.

Using Prompts to Set up Your Essay

You will have 30 minutes to complete each of two essays on the prompts you are given. The prompts can be on just about any topic, but they will follow a predictable pattern in which you are given a statement and then are asked to complete three tasks. The statements are usually philosophical in nature, but sometimes take a stance on a topical issue or controversy. The statement introduces the main idea on which you will need to write. Those three tasks follow the pattern of "thesis/antithesis/synthesis," a common way to analyze an issue.

The first task will always be to explain what the given statement means; this is the thesis part of the analysis. The wording of the second and third tasks will vary from prompt to prompt, as some will be quite specific to the statement given. However, the second task will generally ask you to consider the opposite point of view of the statement you were given, usually by explaining a specific counterexample or counterargument; this is the antithesis part. Finally, the third task will ask you to explain your own point of view on the issue. This is the synthesis part, as you are synthesizing the information given and creating your own position on the issue.

For the sake of simplicity, you should write your essay following the thesis/antithesis/synthesis format, with one paragraph devoted to each task. That will put your essay at three paragraphs, which is admittedly shorter than the five-paragraph essays you may have learned to write in school. However, do not let this make you uncomfortable. First, each paragraph should be of considerable length (they should also all three be of roughly the same length). Plus, three full paragraphs is enough to do in half an hour.

When you write your MCAT essay, you will use the first paragraph to explain what the prompt means, the second to introduce a statement that argues against the prompt (counterargument), and a third to determine whether the prompt is true or false. This means that your usual essay structure of introduction, body, and conclusion will be let go to a certain extent. Think of that three-paragraph or five-paragraph essay you learned in school as only one type; this is a somewhat different format. Take a look at the following example prompt:

Assisted suicide is a highly controversial subject but an important option for the terminally ill.

Write an essay in which you perform the following: Explain the meaning of the above statement. Describe a specific instance where assisted suicide is not an important option for the terminally ill. Discuss whether you believe assisted suicide should be an option available to terminally ill patients.

How to Write an Essay

In practicing for the essay part of the MCAT, you should be creating a step-by-step process that you will be so familiar with by test day that you will write the essays out of habit. The basic process of quickly writing an MCAT essay is:

1. Brainstorm your prompt and its counterargument	2 minutes
2. Write an outline	2 minutes
3. Write a paragraph defining and explaining your prompt	8 minutes
4. Write a paragraph introducing and explaining your counterargument or counterexample	8 minutes
5. Write a paragraph that proves the prompt either true or false	8 minutes
6. Edit your essay for grammar and logic	2 minutes

Brainstorming

You will not have much time in which to explain your position, but you will be expected to do so in detail. Just because you have a simple essay structure and a limited amount of time does not mean you can be vague in your discussion of the prompt and counterargument. Organize your thoughts clearly *before* you begin to write. When you start to write, you should have a clear idea of the beginning, middle, and end of your essay. If you have no idea where you are going, your essay will wander and suffer in coherence.

The first two steps in brainstorming what will be in your essay are pretty straightforward. First you will need to come up with an explanation of what the statement means, Jot down some ideas of how you will explain what the statement means. That is, you need to restate your prompt and define it. Think of your prompt as a very general subject. Your essay fits into that subject, but on a much smaller scale. The simplest way to do this is to restate your prompt in different ways or write down different facts or arguments for and against it.

Start brainstorming facts and arguments using the previous prompt: Assisted suicide is a highly controversial subject, but an important option for the terminally ill. For example:

- Assisted suicide is illegal in most states.
- Assisted suicide is considered immoral in some religions but is an acceptable response to terminal illness in others.

Now look at why assisted suicide is used and why it is controversial:

- Assisted suicide is considered for those whose lives have become unbearable through extreme pain or other considerations. Usually, but not always, these individuals are terminally ill.

- Assisted suicide excites controversy because of cultural and religious taboos against self-destruction.

- Also concerns that vulnerable patients may be euthanized against their wishes or manipulated into agreeing to suicide.

Next you will be expected to give a counterargument, or antithesis. The counterargument is a statement that introduces an argument that is the opposite of the one given in the prompt; it is an argument that assumes the given one is false. Then, list out any ideas or examples you might use to support this statement. For example, in this case, your counterargument could be: Assisted suicide is not a real option because those who would "use" it are often not in a position to make the decision themselves.

- Even if they made the decision in a living will, they may have changed their minds but cannot express that change.

- The mentally ill also are not equipped to make this decision.

- Some may feel depressed due to pain management issues when they decide to pursue assisted suicide and might change their mind when those issues subside.

- To help those mentioned above to kill themselves is murder.

- Use an example of Alzheimer's patient who said she wanted assisted suicide before her dementia set in.

In the third paragraph, you make a choice. You must pick the prompt or the counterargument and prove it true. In other words, you will take a position and argue whether the prompt is true or false. This is the moment where your most important brainstorming begins. You do not necessarily have to pick the side with which you actually agree. Instead, take a minute to list out some arguments you might use on either side, then choose to support the one that seems the easiest to argue for effectively.

Mastering the MCAT

Unless you can come up with strong arguments against the prompt, stick with proving the prompt true. You will generally be able to find more arguments in favor of the prompt than against it. You will need your main counterargument for the middle part of your essay, but you may find yourself coming up with only one. That is all right. When determining this sort of thing, go with the easiest route that allows you to present a detailed, comprehensive essay.

In this example, assume you choose to prove the prompt true. Your task lies in showing not only why the prompt is true, but also why the counterargument does not prove it false. In this case, you acknowledge that the counterargument has, merit but not enough to disprove the prompt. For example, you might say: Despite the concerns, assisted suicide protects a fundamental right for the terminally ill and those suffering from a permanent lack of quality of life — the right to die with dignity. Finally, you should list out some reasons to support your position. Some of these you might already have listed out when you were deciding which side of the argument you should support. Here are some reasons you might use in support of assisted suicide:

- Assisted suicide is a fundamental right for the terminally ill because they are suffering from a permanent lack of quality of life.

- Some will suffer agonizing and prolonged deaths if they are not given the option of assisted suicide.

- The ability to die peacefully is part of enjoying a high quality of life. (use details of the suffering some endure in their last days).

- Medical advances have allowed people to live longer and with more debilitating illnesses, ironically allowing them to suffer more at the end of their lives.

Writing your outline

Now, you need to write an outline. For your essay, you will need three things:

1.	A good definition of and explanation of the statement in the prompt.
2.	A solid antithesis or counterargument to the statement.
3.	Reasons (usually at least three) to support your interpretation of the idea at hand.

To make your outline, you will pull together the best of the arguments you came up with while brainstorming. So, an outline might look like this:

1. **Thesis: Assisted suicide is a highly controversial subject but an important option for the terminally ill.**

    a. Assisted suicide is illegal in most states.

    b. Assisted suicide is considered for those whose lives have become unbearable through extreme pain and/or other considerations. Usually, but not always, these individuals are terminally ill.

    c. Assisted suicide excites controversy because of cultural and religious taboos against self-destruction.

    d. Also concerns that vulnerable patients may be euthanized against their wishes or manipulated into agreeing to suicide.

2. **Antithesis: Assisted suicide is not a real option because those who would "use" it are often not in a position to make the decision themselves.**

   a. Even if they made the decision in a living will, they may have changed their minds but cannot express that change.

   b. The mentally ill also are not equipped to make this decision.

   c. Some may feel depressed due to pain management issues when they decide to pursue assisted suicide, and might change their mind when those issues subside.

   d. To help those mentioned above to kill themselves is murder.

3. **Synthesis: Despite the concerns, assisted suicide protects a fundamental right for the terminally ill and those suffering from a permanent lack of quality of life — the right to die with dignity.**

   a. Assisted suicide is a fundamental right for the terminally ill because they are suffering from a permanent lack of quality of life.

   b. Some will suffer agonizing and prolonged deaths if they are not given the option of assisted suicide.

   c. Medical advances have allowed people to live longer and with more debilitating illnesses, ironically allowing them to suffer more at the end of their lives.

Writing the essay

As you start actually writing your essay, remember the three goals in your essay:

My Goals

1.	Introduce and define the prompt.
2.	Introduce the counterargument or counterexample.
3.	Prove or disprove the prompt.

If you have followed the steps so far, you have already started writing. Some outlines will be more polished than others, but in most cases it will actually save time to just build your essay out of your outline, using the phrases and sentences you have already written and filling them in with more explanation. To see how you might do that, go back to the prompt: "Assisted suicide is a highly controversial subject but an important option for the terminally ill." Your first goal in writing an essay for the MCAT is to further explain and define this sentence. Just because the prompt is vague does not mean that your definition of it can be vague. In fact, a good way to get going on your essay is to define the term you are dealing with in more detail. For example, your definition of assisted suicide should be more sophisticated that the statement you were given, which is true, but it does not say much. Try something more in depth like the following.

Assisted suicide is the act of committing suicide with the help of another person because the individual in question cannot complete the act on his or her own due to advanced illness. This illness is usually terminal in nature and often involves extreme pain. The assisted suicide movement is a highly controversial one. Assisted suicide is considered immoral in some religions but is an acceptable response to terminal illness in others. Despite the legalization of the act in some states, it is illegal in most states.

In the latter example, the paragraph gives a definition of assisted suicide, as well as explaining why the prompt presents this term as highly controversial. It also gives the term and conflict that is referenced a distinct context (present-day United States). One of the biggest mistakes in writing an essay, especially one targeted to a standardized test like the MCAT, is to give no appropriate context for your discussion of the prompt. Avoid beginning sentences with phrases like "since the beginning of time" or "humankind has always..." as these will not begin your essay either strongly or impressively. Test evaluators want to know how the prompt applies to the situation of today, not Egypt 5,000 years ago, and the 6 billion people on this planet are far too large and diverse a group to be an appropriate single example for your essay.

From there, you will finish up your first paragraph by giving more information about the controversy surrounding assisted suicide. This paragraph includes many of the ideas we listed in the outline, but it also fills them in with more ideas and transitions between the ideas so that it flows. It introduces the statement set up in the prompt. That is the first task. Then it defines the term in the prompt (assisted suicide), explains why it is controversial, and why it is an important option for the terminally ill. Here is an example of how you might complete the first paragraph:

Assisted suicide is a highly controversial subject, but an important option for the terminally ill. It excites controversy in the United States due to religious and cultural prohibitions against suicide and concerns about the vulnerability of individuals who opt for it. However, it remains an attractive option for those who are terminally ill or who suffer from debilitating pain or chronic illness. The most controversial aspect of assisted suicide is that those who are likely to want it can no longer physically or mentally complete the act of suicide themselves. Therefore, they require assistance from another party. When the patient gives clear consent, this is somewhat unproblematic. But when the individual is incapable of giving clear consent, this creates more problems. Documents such as living wills can dictate what an individual wants done under such circumstances, but even then, people can change their minds, or loved ones close to them can claim that they have since changed their minds or would have wanted to remain living under this specific circumstance.

Now, let us look at the second paragraph. In this paragraph, you will introduce the counterargument. In a way, you have already done this by discussing the controversy of assisted suicide, which gives a clear transition to the second paragraph. Here, you have the tasks of introducing the counterargument and giving an example supporting it. Here, you are arguing that assisted suicide is not a real option because those who are being assisted cannot give informed consent, and that any prior informed consent is negated by the fact that the person may change his or her mind when faced by the actual situation. This example argues that assisted suicide cannot be an important option for the terminally ill because it is too exploitative for those who would qualify for the option.

Assisted suicide is not a real option because those who would use it are often not in a position to make the decision themselves. Assisted suicide is a misnomer in that it implies that anyone can help another person commit suicide. Many of those who are assisted in killing themselves are so vulnerable they are completely unable to express their wishes on the subject, so the decision is made for them. Even if they have made this decision in the past with a living will, they may have changed their minds but are unable to say so. Thus, this is not assisted suicide at all, but murder. A similar thing goes for those who are mentally ill or otherwise unfit to make such a decision, yet may be considered legally fit to do so. Again, those who are severely depressed due to pain management issues might feel differently about killing themselves if their pain could be brought under control. To help such a person kill him- or herself instead of helping that person learn how to manage his or her pain would also be murder.

Finally, you will need to discuss whether the prompt is true or false. You have already chosen to support the option of assisted suicide, and you have detailed several examples that you might use. Now, you just need to smooth them out into a complete paragraph. The third section discusses the pros and cons of the prompt. It picks a side — that assisted suicide is a fundamental right — and proves that the prompt is true and why. You can argue that the prompt is false, but may be more difficult to do than arguing that the prompt is true. Always go for the easier option that gets the job done, especially for something like the writing sample section, where writing a great essay as opposed to a competent one is not critically important to your passing the MCAT.

Despite the concerns, assisted suicide protects a fundamental right for the terminally ill and those suffering from a permanent lack of quality of life — the right to die with dignity. Assisted suicide is a controversial subject for reasons both cultural and inherent to the basic idea. In the West, suicide is considered the crime of self-murder and is illegal, though it is acceptable and even favored as a solution to certain problems in other cultures, such as that of Japan. It is also controversial because of the issue of consent. Can those being assisted give informed consent when many of them are not of sound mind and body when the assistance becomes necessary? However, there is also the concern that those suffering from terminal illnesses face agonizing and prolonged deaths if they are not given the option of assisted suicide. They might then feel forced to kill themselves while they are still fit enough to do so, which would further shorten their lives. It speaks to the question of what constitutes quality of life. Medical advances in the past few decades have made it possible to maintain a person's body long after any quality of life is gone. People who are brain dead, for example, can be kept on life support for years, even decades. These advances have also ensured that some people who would otherwise have died sooner can be kept alive, but at the cost of being in unspeakable pain. Therefore, there is the question of whether we can unequivocally ban assisted suicide when it can act as a critical counterweight to the potential abuse of medical technology to prolong life. The living will is a concept that exists in the first place to allow people to express their wishes on the subject while they are still considered legally able to do so. As such, the concept of assisted suicide is very important despite being so controversial because it balances an equally controversial subject: the use and abuse of medical technology to prolong life past the point of providing quality of life. This balance is worth preserving.

Editing the essay

Save two minutes or so once you finish your essay for editing. Clearly, you will not be able to do a total revamp in this time. However, you can improve your essay significantly in a short period of time just by finding and fixing errors and making other small improvements.

Mastering the MCAT

As you edit your essay, try to make small improvements to the flow of your writing by adding transition words. These words help the reader transition smoothly from one idea to another and show the relationship between ideas. Examples of transition words are "and," "in addition," "but", "however," "despite," "because," "in consequence," and "therefore."

Writing tips

Now that you have the basic process down, you can work on fine-tuning your essay using the tips below. Practicing will help you work these tips into your routine so that you are not trying to remember them on test day.

1. Remember your audience

One of the most common mistakes among essay writers is forgetting the audience. Here, your audience will be two graders who will evaluate your essay in a very short period of time. They will expect a professional, objective tone from a prospective scientist. Keep in mind that this test comes from an American organization and is for entry into American and Canadian medical schools. The prompts will therefore usually reflect North American current events.

2. Avoid weak arguments

When setting up your counterargument, make sure it is a solid one. Whatever you choose to do, avoid setting up a straw man argument. This is an argument that no rational person would ever hold. Such an argument is so easy to refute that it makes no sense for anyone to hold it. This is why it is called a straw man argument — it can be knocked down as easily as a person made of straw. In the assisted suicide article, a straw man argument might be that supporters of assisted suicide are murderers seeking cover for their actions; this is not going to be a strong argument. Such straw man arguments can be effective rhetorical devices, as discussed in Chapter 8, the verbal reasoning chapter, but they have no place in your MCAT essays.

You also want to avoid preaching to the choir, which is the opposite of the straw man argument in that you present an argument as if it is a given and irrefutable and anyone who disagreed with it would have to be a fool to do so. The phrase comes from the sermons that Christian ministers or priests give from the pulpit. The choir is usually apt to agree with the minister or priest, so preaching to them requires little persuasion. It is far more persuasive to aim one's arguments at the congregation, sitting in the church who are more likely to be skeptical.

3. Watch out for imprecise terminology

The prompts are deliberately vague to force you to do the work of narrowing down your response yourself and giving your personal answer to the prompt instead of something regurgitated or memorized. As such, you will find yourself having to define such nebulous ideas as democracy, politics, scientific ethics, and technology. Keep any such definitions narrow and specific to your approach. You might find it useful to memorize specific definitions of terms that you find in your practice tests and sets, as well as specific examples from history and current events. For example, stating that Marie Curie was a famous female scientist is vague and unimpressive. Saying that Marie Curie was the only person to win the Nobel Prize in two different fields of science or that Curie was a victim of cancer due to her long-term exposure to radioactive isotopes during her experiments is more clear and specific. It also gives you more to work with when presenting examples and fitting them into your arguments and essay overall.

Mastering the MCAT

Do not be afraid to use facts that you are not 100 percent sure are correct; if you are in the ballpark, the graders will not take off points for inaccuracies. However, you do not want to spout out facts that are way off in left field.

4. Always use formal language

Formal essays require a use of formal writing. There are certain things you should definitely avoid in your essay:

- Avoid using popular Internet and text messaging slang.
    Example: Ur happiest when ur @ home

- Do not use offensive language. This includes swear words, racial or religious slurs, and sexist or homophobic terms.

- Use contractions sparingly or not at all.

- Avoid cultural dialect.
    Example: When do y'all reckon supper will be ready?

- Avoid wording that is too casual.
    Example: The President of the United States is a really good guy.

- Do not use first-person point of view.
  Example: I think that abortion should be legal.

- Avoid highly emotive arguments.
  Example: Anybody who thinks that nuclear power is a good idea is stupid.

- Avoid using personal anecdotes.
  Example: We decided to take my grandmother off life support on the advice of her doctors. I still believe that this decision was wrong.

Formal language helps to establish you as a serious speaker — someone who is an expert on the subject of your prompt even when you are not. Tone, as you may have already noticed in the section on verbal reasoning in Chapter 8, is extremely important.

5. Keep it impersonal

Even though it is a very specific type of writing, the MCAT essay is still a formal one. Using "I," personal anecdotes, or other personal examples is not appropriate for the MCAT; you should discuss the prompt from a distant and objective perspective. Even though you are giving your opinion, you are basing this opinion on facts, so you are expected to argue based on logic and rational thought processes not emotion. Arguing based on emotion or personal attack reduces your credibility rather than enhances it and also reduces the effectiveness of your essay. While you do not want to bore the grader, you need not spend too much time on making your essay pretty or elegant. The main point of your essay is to explain the prompt and support or refute it. That is all. You will not lose points for putting it in a less-than-fascinating fashion, as long as it is clear and does the job.

Writing Section Practice Exercises

Now it is time for you to practice writing MCAT essays using the sample prompts below. Be sure to time yourself, using no more than 30 minutes to complete each of the three prompts below, using the following steps:

1.	Restate the prompt in your own words.
2.	Write three reasons why the prompt is true, and three reasons why it is false.
3.	Write a counterargument for each prompt.
4.	Write the first paragraph that includes the introduction, restatement of the prompt, and definitions of any terms.
5.	Write a second paragraph to introduce and explain your counterargument, or the antithesis. Use some of the ideas from your list of why the statement is false.
6.	Write a final paragraph for each prompt stating whether it is true or false and why. If stating that it is true, explain why the antithesis is false. Use more of your reasons from Step 2.

After you complete the first essay, you can evaluate your performance by comparing your essay to the example essays on that prompt in the back of the book. You should also read the analyses of each sample essay to see if you made the same mistakes those writers did. From there, you can gauge your own improvement on the second and third essays.

Mastering the MCAT

Practice essay examples are good to study to ensure that you understand what is expected on the MCAT essays. When you look up the sample essays on these prompts, you will find examples of low-, medium-, and high-score essays. Study them carefully and emulate the high-scoring ones as much as possible as you practice writing essays.

Prompt 1: Civil disobedience is the best response to unfair laws.

Write an essay in which you do the following: Explain the meaning of the above statement. Describe a specific instance where civil disobedience is not the best response to unfair laws. Discuss what you think determines when civil disobedience is an appropriate/inappropriate response.

Prompt 2: Abortion is a woman's right to choose.

Write an essay in which you do the following: Explain the meaning of the above statement. Describe a specific instance where abortion should not be a choice. Discuss whether abortion is a woman's right to choose.

Prompt 3: A government should never spend more than it takes in.

Write an essay in which you do the following: Explain the meaning of the above statement. Describe a specific instance where a government should spend more than it takes in. Discuss whether a government should spend more than it takes in.

chapter 10

Biological Sciences

The biological sciences section covers two main areas: biology and organic chemistry. This section consists of 52 multiple-choice questions in seven to nine sets with ten to 13 questions each. It is scored, like the other multiple-choice sections, on a scale from 1 to 15. Most of the questions (around 80 percent) are biology questions. The testing time lasts 70 minutes.

While the physical sciences chapter is nearly evenly split between physics and chemistry — and features many questions that test both disciplines — the biological sciences chapter is much more heavily skewed toward biology. Organic chemistry questions are less common than the biology questions, and more often than not you will be able to identify them as chemistry questions. Notice that the biological sciences section, the most pertinent section to your future in medicine, comes last. This is probably not a coincidence. The MCAT seems to save the best for last, but being last means that you might not be at your best when you get to the biological sciences section. On the other hand, the biological sciences section has much overlap with the physical sciences section, in that you will find yourself using physics and chemistry, in addition to biology.

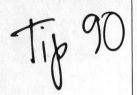

Mastering the MCAT

Having the biological sciences section come last means that you will not lose your focus on the test by taking the other sections afterward. But it also means that you will not have the same energy for this section as you did for the others, especially since you just had a section where you read articles and analyzed them, and another where you wrote two essays. Be sure to pace yourself and use your breaks to snack or otherwise attend to your physical needs. Stretch and try to clear your mind before you tackle this section.

Tackling the Biological Sciences Section

Chapter 6 reviewed general guidelines for completing the physical sciences and biological sciences sections. For the biology section, however, there are other guidelines to consider. Generally speaking, the organic chemistry questions you will encounter in the biological sciences section look a lot more like the problems in the physical sciences section. The biology questions, however, are quite different. They tend to be longer than the organic chemistry questions, involve reading more information that may not be directly relevant to the question, and require more reading comprehension. They are also focused more on systems of mammalian biology and facts, whereas the organic chemistry questions — as well as the entire physical sciences section — are focused more on equations, chemical processes, and laboratory techniques.

Mastering the MCAT

Keep in mind that most of the questions will be based on biology. This does not mean that you should neglect the organic chemistry questions, but it can help you keep the proper perspective in answering them. Do not spend all of your time practicing organic chemistry questions, when those questions will only consist of about 20 percent of this section. Balance your time management during your study to reflect this.

You should therefore approach the biological sciences section somewhat differently from other sections. Here, you are required to use different, almost opposite, skills within the same section. You must use almost as many reading comprehension skills in the biology questions as you must for the verbal reasoning section, albeit for a different purpose than in the verbal reasoning section. In the verbal reasoning section, you are being tested on your analytical and logic skills, whereas in the biology questions, you are being tested on your knowledge of the various branches of biology. However, in the organic chemistry questions, you will use skills relevant to chemistry, and involving techniques that you learned in the laboratory.

First, practice the questions in the same manner that you will receive them by doing mixed sets with the types of problems you will see in this section. Practice always helps, but in this case, it helps you learn how to deal with the switch between the different types of analysis involved in the two types of questions. Learn the best way for you to handle them.

Practice time management

As always, you need to maintain a good balance of time management on the test. This will be harder to do in the biological sciences section than it will be in other sections because you must restrict the amount of time you spend reading the biology material. Biology questions involve a lot of reading, whereas organic chemistry questions are usually stripped down to the question itself and a list of equations from which to choose your answer.

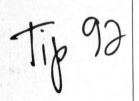

Mastering the MCAT

Rather than read the biology passages thoroughly, trying to soak up every detail, you should focus on the relevant points and data, just as you should do with the passages in the verbal reasoning section. Then, in the organic chemistry questions, you must remember not to insert information that is not there already. This may seem obvious, but these are different skills, and you will need to practice both.

Nor should you want to waste too much time on one set or the other. Just because you decide to answer one type of question because you find it easier does not mean that you should take more time over it. If anything, you should restrict the time that you spend on the questions that you find easy. For example, the biology questions tend to have more information than you absolutely need to answer the question. You can easily get wrapped up in the passage by trying to get it all down. If you do not like reading, you are more likely to read slowly in the first place, and read even more slowly to make sure that you do not miss anything. Do not underestimate the ability of large passages of text to strike fear into the heart of a test taker at the wrong moment.

Conversely, the organic chemistry questions can seem foreboding to someone who gets information more readily from reading than from equations. That person may find the arrangement bewildering and intimidating, and might linger over the question because he or she does not know where to begin.

Pacing and time management, in both the practice sessions and the MCAT itself, are critical skills to learn for the biological sciences section. Make at least one plan beforehand during your practice sessions regarding how you will deal with this mix of questions and information delivery types so that you will not break stride when dealing with them.

Mastering the MCAT

It is easy to become stuck inside your comfort zone and avoid the questions you find difficult because they make you uncomfortable. Instead, go through your comfort zone as quickly as you can without missing important information or making unnecessary errors so you will have more time in which to deal with the uncomfortable things.

Skip carefully

Because these questions involve different skills, consider answering them out of order. You may, for example, decide to answer the organic chemistry questions in order and then the biology questions in order, or vice versa. You should determine during your review which type is easier for you. There are a couple of potential risks in skipping around, however. You do not want to confuse yourself and lose track of what questions you have already answered. When in doubt, always answer the question and move on. You can always go back to it if you have time, and if you run out of time, at least you have put down an answer that may be right.

However, you should not jump around from question to question randomly. That is a quick way of ending up with a half-finished section and dropping questions you might have answered and gotten credit for. If you skip a question, note it down so that you will know to go back to it. If you answer a question before you have had time to properly determine the answer (or you guessed with no real idea of the answer), note that down, too, so that you will not waste time going back over the section to determine what questions you might have missed or been shaky about. Use your scratch paper for this on the practice tests and real test.

Keep your motivation

Keep in mind that no matter how much time you schedule during your practice sessions for the end of each section, you will probably end up with less than you had planned, or even none at all. This is most true in a section like biological sciences where you are being thrown more than one type of question with more than one type of learning. Things come up. Questions throw you off-track. You find yourself straying off your timeline, particularly toward the end of the test when you are already tired and only wanting to finish and leave. Learn to roll with these issues and you will do better than if you fight them.

For example, you can use your impatience to finish the MCAT at this point in the test to your advantage if you remain disciplined. Remind yourself that this is near the end and adopt a no-nonsense approach to the reading. Concentrate only on finding the things that seem relevant. This may actually be easier than at the beginning of the test, when everything is new and seems to merit intense concentration. By the end of the test, you just want to finish and leave. So focus on the things that will ensure you make this goal as thoroughly as necessary. Just remember that you will also be inclined to use shortcuts and get sloppy — that you must avoid. Remember that the longer you can stay sharp, the sooner you can leave. That may seem like a contradiction, but it is true that the sloppier you are, the more time you will need to take to answer the questions.

What You Need to Know About Biology

For biology, you can assume one thing based on the ultimate goal of the MCAT: You will mostly be asked questions that relate to human biology. You are studying and testing to become a physician, not an oceanographer or a veterinarian. You should therefore expect a focus that suits this goal. The MCAT does not expect you to know high levels of medicine, but that does not mean you will not get any questions pertaining to medical issues. Studying for the biology part of the MCAT pulls you away from numbers and formulas into an area of science where your success will be based more on having a firm grasp of biological concepts. First, you need to know a few basic things about the human body, such as the structures of the cell and disease organisms such as bacteria and viruses. You will also find questions on cellular biology, microbiology, prokaryotes, and eukaryotes. Molecular biology has more to do with the processes of the body, both normal and abnormal.

Molecular biology

For molecular biology, you should know the basic structures of the cell, in addition to processes such as osmosis and concepts such as the difference between DNA and RNA.

Words to know

Cell wall	A membrane that surrounds a cell, protecting it and giving it a rigid outer exterior. Plants have call walls, but animals do not.
Osmosis	One of several processes that involve the transfer of substances across cell walls or membranes; osmosis involves the transfer of a solvent, usually water.
Nucleolus	The structure within the nucleus of a cell serves as the brain of the cell; it contains the RNA of the cell.
Chromosomes	Structures in the nucleus that contain the DNA necessary for cell life and division.

Cytoplasm	The fluid that maintains the structure of the cell and facilitates transfer of nutrients.
Mitochondria	The "engines" of the cell that produce food from basic building blocks of glucose and oxygen.
RNA	Messenger DNA that transmits messages inside a cell.
DNA	These double-helix strands are called the building blocks of life because they contain the genetic information that controls cell growth, division, and function.
Amino acids	The building blocks of protein; they contain a basic amino (NH_2) group, an acidic carboxyl (COOH) group, and a side chain attached to an alpha carbon atom. Both DNA and RNA are made up of amino acids.
Cell division	This process occurs when a cell splits into two cells, known as "daughter cells."

Concepts to know

- **The difference between the two basic types of cell division, mitosis and meiosis:** In the case of mitosis, the cell divides into two identical daughter cells. In the case of meiosis, the cell divides into cells that are not identical to the original cell. Different areas of the body contain different types of cells; mitosis is the more common, while meiosis occurs in the reproductive structures of the body.

- **Ways in which a cell can be damaged:** Include radiation (by ionizing the atoms of a cell) and chemical damage (by the introduction of toxic substances). Either type of damage can lead to organ failure and death.

- **Mechanisms that cause metabolic diseases such as cancer:** Genes that stimulate normal cell growth can be converted to cancerous cells through UV radiation, chemicals, or mutations.

- **Types of cells and the structures with which they are associated:** Red blood cells are created in the bone marrow and spleen; white blood cells are created in the lymph system.

The nervous system

Much of the MCAT biology section relates to the body's various systems, which are all important. The nervous system plays a big role in the MCAT, perhaps due to its applications in managing pain in the practice of medicine.

Words to know

Nerves	Bundles of fibers that transmit impulses between nerve centers and the parts of the body.
Neurons	The basic cells of nerves; neurons receive nervous impulses and send output to the parts of the body. They are made up of dendrites (receptive surfaces), a single axon (which carries materials from the cell body to synapses), and a single cell body.
Synapse	The junction between neurons across which impulses are transmitted chemically or electrically between cells to drive the nervous system.
Neurotransmitter	A substance that travels across the synaptic cleft or the space between nerve cells, to transmit information.
Acetylcholine	A common neurotransmitter, this chemical carries information between nerve cells.

Concepts to know

- **Three parts of the nervous system:**

  a. Central nervous system, including the brain and spinal cord.

  b. Autonomic nervous system, involving involuntary processes and reflexes such as breathing and heart rate.

  c. Voluntary nervous system, including the movement of limbs. There is some crossover between the voluntary and autonomic systems; for example, you can learn to control your breathing, and even your heart rate, through biofeedback techniques, but they will continue without having to pay attention to them.

- **The different structures of the brain:**

  a. Cerebrum, which regulates higher functions.

  b. Cerebellum, which regulates lower functions such as basic emotions and hormones.

  c. Medulla, which regulates autonomic functions such as breathing and heart rate.

  d. Medulla oblongata, which is brain stem.

  e. Hypothalamus, which regulates sleep, temperature, and sexual development, as well as the functions of the pituitary gland.

- **Membranes of the brain:** The pia mater is the thin, innermost membrane surrounding the brain, from which it gets blood; dura mater is the tough outer membrane that protects the brain and spinal cord.

The musculoskeletal system

This crucial system includes the skeleton and muscles, as well as connecting tissues such as tendons. You will also need to be familiar with the major bone structures and muscle groups.

Words to know

Muscle	A tissue that generates force by contracting its cells using one of several mechanisms, such as body movement and generating heat.
Skeletal muscle	One of the three types of muscle, it connects to bones via tendons.
Cardiac muscle	This type of muscle makes up most of the heart.

Smooth muscle	This type of muscle is found in blood vessels, the intestine, and the uterus.
Bones	Hard, calcified tissue that makes up the skeleton of humans and other vertebrates.
Tendons	Tissues that connect muscles to bones. The connections can take longer to heal than either of the systems, which is why a strain or sprain (overstretching or ripping of the fibers of a tendon) can be more damaging and take longer to heal than a bone fracture.
Joints	The interconnections between bones. They are held together by ligaments and are moved by muscles.
Skin	An organ that protects internal organs, creates vitamin D, and helps regulate body temperature, among other functions.

Concepts to know

- **The process of muscle contraction:** Nerves transmit electrical impulses that move muscles. Muscle contraction begins when a neuron attaches to a muscle cell, releasing a neurotransmitter into a muscle cell. From there, action potential moves deep into the muscle tissue via small tunnels called T-tubules.

- **Muscles can move voluntarily or involuntarily:** This depends on the nerves that are attached to them. Skeletal muscle is voluntary muscle tissue, while cardiac muscle is involuntary muscle tissue. Smooth muscle is mainly involuntary.

- **Function of bone:** Bone is a living tissue that supports soft tissue, protects internal organs, helps in body movement, and stores energy and nutrients.

- **Bone structures and muscle groups:**
  a. Cranium, which are the bones of the skill.
  b. Spine, including cervical, thoracic, lumbar, sacrum, and coccyx.

c. Large arm and leg bones, including humerus, radius/ulna for the arms, femurs, and tibia/fibula for the legs.

d. Hands and feet, including carpals, metacarpals, tarsals, and metatarsals.

e. Ribs cage, including 24 ribs connecting to the sternum.

f. Pelvis, including the sacrum and pubic bone.

The cardiovascular and respiratory systems

The cardiovascular system (also known as the circulatory system) centers around the muscle known as the heart, which will play a major role in any MCAT questions dealing with this system. The pulmonary system is intimately connected to the circulatory system, so we will go over the key concepts in both systems together.

Words to know

Heart	A powerful organ that draws in blood from the extremities and pumps it back out after passing it through the lungs and oxygenating it. Other parts of the cardiovascular system include arteries, capillaries, and veins.
Arteries	Muscular vessels through which blood goes out to the extremities.
Capillaries	Peripheral vessels that diffuse oxygen and nutrients directly to the cells.
Veins	Vessels that conduct blood and waste products back to the heart.
Pulmonary (or respiratory) system	This system draws in oxygen through air into the lungs and diffuses it to the blood vessels of the circulatory system and the heart, which then pumps it out to the arteries. The blood vessels also diffuse carbon dioxide out as a metabolic waste, and this is exhaled by the lungs.

Concepts to know

- **Structure of the heart:** The heart has four chambers. Though you will normally not need to know very much about the body structures of other animals, you should know the differences between a human heart and that of lower life forms — specifically, how many chambers it has and why. For example, fish have only two chambers; amphibians and reptiles have three.

- **Major diseases of the heart and circulatory system:** These include arteriosclerosis and stroke.

- **Parts of the pulmonary system:** These include macrostructures like the lungs, trachea, and bronchi, and microstructures like the bronchioles and alveoli.

- **The mouth and nose are also parts of the pulmonary system:** Parts of the nose include nasal passages and sinuses, while the tonsils, larynx, and pharynx are all parts of the mouth. These structures facilitate human speech and put up barriers to disease and foreign objects or other obstructions, such as water.

- **Major diseases of the pulmonary system:** These include pneumonia (literally, fluid in the lungs), pulmonary embolism, chronic obstructive pulmonary disease (COPD), and emphysema.

Tip 94

Mastering the MCAT

The division into more chambers with strong walls and valves separating them makes for a more powerful organ, which allows warm-bloodedness.

The digestive and excretory systems

The digestive system is one of the most complex macrosystems in the body, though the MCAT does not cover the system in great detail. The digestive system is closely related to the excretory system, which is why they are covered together.

Words to know

Stomach	The central organ of the digestive system; the stomach is a muscular bag used for storing and churning food. The main cell types in the stomach include mucous cells, peptic (chief) cells, parietal (oxyntic) cells, and G cells.
The small intestine	The organ where most digestion and absorption of food occurs; it is about 3 meters long.
The large intestine	Also known as the colon; it is responsible for water and electrolyte absorption.
Digestion	The process by which food is broken down so that it can be used as energy. Various hormones, such as gastrin and secretin, assist in this process.
Absorption	The process by which nutrients such as carbohydrates, proteins, and fats are processed for use by individual cells.

Concepts to know

- **The function of the digestive system:** To break down food so that it can be used as energy.

- **Parts of the digestive tract involved in digesting solids:** The mouth, esophagus, stomach, small intestine, and large intestine (including the colon, the rectum, and the anus).

- **Parts of the digestive tract involved in digesting liquids:** The esophagus, stomach, kidneys, bladder, and urethra.

- **Structures that contribute to the digestive system but are not connected to it:** Gall bladder, which contributes bile to the stomach, and the liver contributes digestive enzymes.

- **Major diseases of the digestive system:** Ulcers or dysentery.

- **Functions of the kidney:** To regulate the level of certain chemicals in the blood and to excrete waste.

The immune system

The immune system consists of many structures in the body, most notably the lymph system, which works to defend the body against infection, disease, and other foreign substances.

Words to know

Lymph system	A series of vessels comparable to blood vessels, but without a strong pump to push it around like the heart. The lymph system exists to take dead cells out of the blood stream and rest of the body.
Lymph nodes	The lymph system isolates and attacks disease using lymphocytes (white blood cells), isolating it in structures called "lymph nodes," which can be found most notably on the neck, under the arms and on the groin.
Pathogens	The invading microorganisms that the immune system seeks to dispel; pathogens are any disease-causing agent that usually come in the form of bacteria or viruses.

Mastering the MCAT

To remember the importance of the lymph system, remember that swelling of the lymph nodes has long been a sign of infection, as in the infamous pandemic of Bubonic Plague during the Black Death of 1347-51 in Europe, when victims' lymph nodes swelled into "bulboes," turned black, and burst. The victims' immune systems were completely overwhelmed by the disease.

Concepts to know

- **Major pathogens:** You will probably get at least some questions asking about pathogens and the body's immune system. Like Bubonic Plague, the infectious diseases with the highest mortality rates — such as Ebola or AIDS — attack the immune system directly and overwhelmingly in some way. Also, diseases such as these have become a popular topic of discussion in medicine in recent decades because their prevalence has increased after several decades of decline of infectious diseases in the West.

- **Where diseases are most successful:** The diseases that actually kill the largest number of people (because of the number of people it infects rather than an especially high mortality rate) tend to be those that enter through the digestive system (such as dysentery, cholera, typhus, and typhoid) or through a direct invasion of the bloodstream (such as malaria, as well as a variety of other insect-borne fevers).

- **Where in the body you can find the immune system:** Most of the body has structures dealing with immunity, most notably in those areas that take in outside materials. Here are some examples:

a. Nose hairs in the nasal passages filter out particles before they reach the trachea and lungs. If they are particularly irritating, they will be expelled via sneezing.

b. Hydrochloric acid in the stomach breaks down food for digestion and kills off many invasive organisms. Polyps in intestines enclose and seal off irritants that make it that far.

c. In the bloodstream, both red blood cells and white blood cells fight off infections, with the white blood cells literally engulfing the invading cells.

The endocrine and reproductive systems

The reproductive system, one of the mainstays of physiology, does not have a large presence on the MCAT, though you should be familiar with the anatomy of the reproductive system and a few other concepts. In contrast, the endocrine system, which deals with hormone chemistry, is a popular one on the MCAT.

Words to know

Thyroid	Produces thyroxin and is found in the neck. It regulates the metabolic processes of the body. Problems with thyroid production can result in hypothyroidism or hyperthyroidism. Both conditions can be misdiagnosed as a bipolar disorder and can cause cardiac problems.
Hypothyroidism	A disease caused by insufficient hormone production; results in lower metabolism, weight gain, and a variety of generalized health problems.
Hyperthyroidism	A disease caused by excessive hormone production by the thyroid; results in higher metabolism, weight loss, and a variety of stress-related problems.
Pituitary gland	Found in the cerebellum. This gland is a "master" gland that produces hormones that "trigger" other organs to produce their own hormones.

Ovaries	Produce estrogen and are found only in women in the lower abdomen, attached to the uterus via the fallopian tubes. There are two ovaries, which also regulate the menstrual cycle. Estrogen is also produced by men, but at lower levels.
Testes	Found only in men, located between the rectum and the penis. They produce testosterone and regulate a man's production of sperm. Testosterone is related to aggression. It is also produced in women, but at lower levels.
Adrenal glands	Regulate metabolism like the thyroid. They produce adrenaline, which triggers the "fight or flight" reflex in stressful situations. They are located on top of the kidneys in the posterior of the body.
Gall bladder	Collects bile to aid in digestion. It is located in the center of the body on top of the large intestine.
Pancreas	Produces enzymes that aid in digestion as well as insulin. Pancreatic malfunctions result in diabetic disorders.

Concepts to know

- **The hormonal system:** An extremely complex network of chemical triggers and signals that regulate the body's processes. Although most organs produce hormones, notable structures that produce hormones that regulate major processes include the thyroid, adrenal glands, liver, pancreas, testes, ovaries, and pituitary gland. These organs interact in a complex and delicate balance, with some hormones turning other hormones on or off.

- **Negative feedback:** This important MCAT concept deals with the tendency of endocrine glands to overproduce hormones, causing other organs to produce inhibitors. While one might logically think that high insulin levels, for instance, cause high glucose, the truth is the reverse — the high glucose levels stimulate the overproduction of insulin.

- **Diseases and disorders related to the endocrine system:** Diabetes (dysfunction of the pancreas), hypothyroidism, and hyperthyroidism (dysfunction of the thyroid).

- **Female reproductive organs:** Uterus, ovaries, fallopian tubes, vagina, vulva, and mammary glands (breasts).

- **Male reproductive organs:** Testes, penis, vas deferens, and scrotum.

Tip 96

Mastering the MCAT

The best way to deal with organic chemistry is to remember what it is: the chemistry of biological interactions, or of interactions of organic compounds. Organic compounds are all based on hydrocarbons, or compounds with a hydrogen and carbon base. Hydrogen and carbon are the basis for organic chemistry. Remembering that organic chemistry is, at its heart, about the many different combinations of hydrocarbon molecules will help you keep these questions straight.

Organic chemistry is not a huge part of the MCAT, but it is an intimidating part, and one that is quite different from others. To help you study for these problems and answer them correctly on the test, here are some hints for dealing with organic chemistry in addition to the words and concepts you will need to know for these questions.

Mastering the MCAT

The MCAT does like to throw the unfamiliar at you. For organic chemistry, you can break the more complex compounds down into more basic groups. Just as you might break down a new word into its component part — root, prefix, and suffix — if you know the basics, you will have a better chance of mastering even the most complex subjects.

When studying for organic chemistry questions, you should remember that most of these questions will be presented as formulas or projections, about which you will be asked questions on topics such as valence, solubility, molecular weight, and other chemical or physical properties of the compound being represented. You may also be asked to determine the end products of an experiment, such as the compounds created or the energy used. Or, you may be asked to determine the identity of groups.

Mastering the MCAT

Organic chemistry can seem incredibly complex, but remember that the various groups you must memorize are built along the same principles. Therefore, to organize your studying, try beginning with the simplest and the most common compounds (these are often the same thing) in each group. Memorize their properties, their various structures and projections, and their most common interactions.

What You Need to Know About Organic Chemistry

Organic chemistry questions do not come in a separate section on the test or in a distinct part of this session. They will be mixed in with the biology questions and will involve some different thinking skills. Organic chemistry questions tend to be about laboratory procedures or visual representations of chemical equations. With the latter, keep in mind that you balance out the equation, just as if it were in stoichiometric or mathematical form. With visual representations, you must count the atoms in the molecules involved and pick the answer that coincides with the number you come up with.

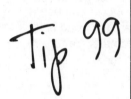

Mastering the MCAT

It is important to remember that not all organic compounds are those found in living tissue. So, what is an organic compound if it is not simply one that is part of a biological process? How can something like motor oil be an organic compound? Petroleum products such as oil, natural gas, gasoline, and coal are all called fossil fuels. They are literally the liquid and fossils of plants and animals from millions of years ago. Geological forces into liquid or rigid solid formations of hydrogen and carbon molecules have squeezed them down.

Molecular structure

The most important organic chemistry topic is subject, as far as the MCAT is concerned, is molecular structure. This will also be the basis of all of the rest of the organic chemistry you will need to know for the test.

Words to know

Valence	Number of bonds that a given atom generally forms.
Structural formulas	Different ways in which molecules can be drawn on paper. There most basic of these is the Lewis structure.

Alkane	A compound that is saturated with hydrogen atoms; the other atoms in the compound have made all the possible bonds that they can with hydrogen atoms, making the compound non-reactive. For this reason, alkanes can sometimes be ignored in MCAT reaction questions.
Isomerism	Occurs when to distinct compounds share a molecular formula.
Sigma-bond (σ-bond)	A highly stable, low-energy type of covalent bond, the sigma-bond is always the first to be formed between two atoms.
Pi-bond (π-bond)	A weaker, higher-energy type of covalent bond, pi-bonds occur when more than one bond is formed. For instance, if two atoms make three bonds, two of them will be pi-bonds.

Concepts to know

- **Index of hydrogen deficiency:** You can determine whether a compound is alkane by calculating its index of hydrogen deficiency, i.e. how many hydrogen atoms it needs in order to become saturated. The equation for a saturated alkane is 2n+2 hydrogens. The variable equals the number of carbon atoms.

  The index of hydrogen deficiency = $[(2n+2) - x]/2$, where n equals the number of carbon atoms and x equals the number of hydrogen atoms. Other elements may be counted as all or part of a hydrogen. One halogen equals one hydrogen and two nitrogens equal one hydrogen. Oxygen atoms are not counted.

Structural formulas to know.

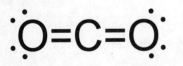

Lewis structure (also known as the Lewis-dot diagram): The nuclei of atoms are represented by their letters on the atomic chart (O for oxygen, C for carbon).

Electron bonds are represented by dots, with each electron represented as a single dot. A single string of dots between letters is a single bond, a double string a double bond, and so on. The number of bonds formed is the "valence" of the atom. The image to the left is the Lewis structure for carbon dioxide (CO_2).

Dash formulas: This is a two-dimensional representation showing which atoms are attached to which, but not the three-dimensional shape of the molecule. For example, a water molecule would look like: H-O-H. They are useful for showing the strength of bonds, but because they only show two dimensions, they reduce the complexity of three-dimensional hydrocarbon molecules.

Condensed formulas: This is the most familiar of the chemical structure formulas. It shows only the symbols and numbers in the molecule for each atom, with the central atoms coming first. Condensed formulas do not show bonds, but they are important because they are the molecule's usual representation in equations, and because the order of the atoms in the condensed formulas also affects their naming. For example, the condensed formula for pentane is: $CH_3CH_2CH_2CH_2CH_3$.

Skeletal (bond-line) formulas: Although the condensed formula is the most common in chemistry, you are more likely to see the bond-line formula on the MCAT. This type of formula looks like angle drawings put together. In it, a carbon atom is assumed at every corner, ending or intersecting the line unless some other element's symbol is placed there. Any hydrogen atoms attached to the carbon atom are assumed. Hydrogen atoms only appear in this formula if they are attached to another type of atom. The image to the left shows the skeletal formula for cyclohexane, C_6H_{12}.

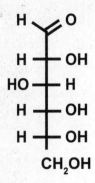

Fischer projections: Also common on the MCAT are Fischer projections, which represent three-dimensional bonds between atoms in two-dimensional form. Any vertical lines represent bonds up and down on the page. Horizontal lines represent bonds that project out of the page at the reader. The Fischer projection represents bonds at right angles along an x-y-z axis, though molecular bonds can actually be on diagonals, as implied by bond-line formulas. The image to the left is the Fischer project for glucose, $C_6H_{12}O_6$.

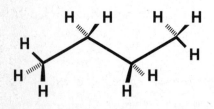

Newman projections: This projection type looks at the molecule along the axis of one of the bonds (rather than from the hypothetically objective angle of other projections). As such, circles and intersections represent carbon atoms (much as in the skeletal formulas). The image to the left shows a Newman projection of butane, C_4H_{10}.

Dash-wedge formulas: This is another three-dimensional representation in two dimensions. Bonds are represented by wedges connecting the carbon and hydrogen atoms. Black projects out of the page (as with horizontal lines in the Fischer projection). Dashed goes along the same plane as the page (as with vertical lines in Fischer). The image to the left shows a dash-wedge formula for butane, C_4H_{10}.

Ball-and-stick models: In these, atoms are represented by differently colored balls. Unlike other formulas, the distance between atoms is made more or less to scale in the ball-and-stick models. The image to the left shows a ball-and-stick model of cyclohexane, C_6H_{12}.

Functional groups

When solving problems in the organic chemistry, you may become confused by all of the conflicting bonds and atoms. Hydrocarbons are often extremely complex. However, you should keep in mind that not all of the atoms that you see require your attention.

Mastering the MCAT

When approaching a confusing organic chemistry problem, you should only concentrate on the groups that are chemically reactive and are not alkane. Because alkanes are non-reactive, you can ignore them in most questions.

Words and concepts to know

The terms below are a listing of the functional groups that you should understand, recognize, and memorize for the MCAT.

Alkanes	Have ten prefixes corresponding to their number of carbons. So, for example, methane has one carbon and butane has four. They have the lowest density of all the groups, and are almost completely insoluble. • 1: meth- • 6: hex- • 2: eth- • 7: hept- • 3: prop- • 8: oct- • 4: but- • 9: non- • 5: pent- • 10: dec-

Alkenes	Also known as olefins in the petroleum industry, alkenes are unsaturated compounds that have at least one single carbon bond. Ethylene (C_2H_4) is the simplest of the alkenes, and other simple alkenes follow a similar format of C_nH_n.
Alkynes	Also known as the "acetylenes" after the compound acetylene (C_2H_2), these compounds have a triple carbon bond. They are generally both less saturated and more reactive than alkenes. Alkynes tend to show up in plants. In medicine, they can be found in antitumor drugs (calicheamicin) and contraceptives (norethynodrel).
Alcohols	This group is most well known for ethanol (drinking alcohol) and methanol (wood alcohol). In alcohols, the carbon atom is bound both with an alkyl (a type of hydrocarbon) or its equivalent and a hydroxide (OH) group. These compounds are often used as industrial solvents, and ethanol is a depressant.
Ethers	An ether group is an oxygen atom attached to an alkyl and an aryl (a functional group derived from a simple aromatic ring): R-O-R. Ethers are used in medicine as solvents and anesthetics.
Amines	A nitrogen atom with a long pair of unbonded electrons. Amines make up amino acids, the basic building blocks of DNA. They are found in many drugs such as antihistamines (Chlorpheniramine), tranquilizers (Chlorpromazine), decongestants (Ephedrine), and antidepressants (amoxapine).
Aldehydes	Contains a terminal carbonyl group; a carbon that is bonded to both a hydrogen and an oxygen atom, such as O = CH-). Aldehydes are also called formyl or methanoyl groups.
Ketones	A group of in which carbonyl is bonded with two other carbon atoms. In humans, ketones are a byproduct of metabolic reactions. They are used as solvents in industry.
Carboxylic acids	Contain the functional group COOH. One type of carboxylic acid you are likely to see on the MCAT is aliphatic acids, or fatty acids. Carboxylic acids have a high boiling point and are soluble in water.

Esters	Created by the interaction between an acid (oxoacid) and an alcohol (hydroxyl). They are quite common, especially as fatty acids in oils. Low molecular weight esters appear in perfume. Others are part of DNA, and still others (like nitro-glycerine) are explosive.
Amides	An amine that is bonded to a carbonyl group (a functional group consisting of a carbon and oxygen atom double-bonded to each other). It has different properties from an amine, however. Amides are weak bases and are about as soluble as esters, but less soluble than comparable amines. Amide bonds are also known as peptide bonds. Amides are frequently drugs, such as LSD and penicillin.
Alkyls	These do not generally appear alone, but do so as part of a more complex molecule. The term refers to any monovalent radical, and methyl is the simplest form.

Mastering the MCAT

One famous amine is the drug amphetamine, an illegal stimulant. Amines can be very biological-ly active, and the larger groups can be beneficial. Smaller amine groups, ones with lower molecu-lar weight, are toxic.

Reactions and products

The next step is to detail some of the reactions you will see within these groups and the products of those reactions. Listed below are the five types of reactions you will see on the MCAT, along with the relevant information about each.

Substitutions	Reactions caused when one functional group replaces another. Two examples are S_N1 reactions, which happen in two steps, and S_N2 reactions, which happen in one step.

Additions	A type of reaction caused when molecules are combined with one another. Examples include hydrogenation and electrophilic addition.
Eliminations	The type of reaction caused when one or more functional groups are removed to form a double bond. Examples include synthesis of an alkene.
Oxidations	Reactions that involve the loss of hydrogen; they are usually caused by agents that contain large amounts of oxygen.
Reductions	Reactions that involve the addition of hydrogen and the loss of oxygen; they are usually caused by agents that contain large amounts of hydrogen.

Key reactions

- **Combustion:** This reaction occurs when oxygen is added to an alkane at a high temperature. The main products of this reaction are carbon dioxide and heat. Combustion is a redox reaction, a combined oxidation and reduction.

- **Halogenation:** A reaction that occurs when halogens react with alkanes in the presence of heat or light, producing free radicals. While it is most often associated with alkanes, alkenes also undergo halogenation.

- **Dehydration of an alcohol:** This is an elimination reaction in which an alcohol reacts to a concentrated acid to produce an alkene. The reverse of this reaction is the hydration of an alkene.

Macromolecules and laboratory techniques

While you will not be expected to know a lot about biochemistry, the MCAT will include questions on the basic properties of macromolecules, including carbohydrates, proteins, lipids, and amino acids. Finally, the

MCAT will expect you to know a handful of laboratory techniques used in organic chemistry.

Major macromolecules

- **Carbohydrates:** Different combinations of carbon and water in which there is one oxygen and two hydrogen atoms for each carbon atom. The ones most likely to be tested on the MCAT are fructose (a ketose) and glucose (an aldehyde).

- **Proteins:** Made up of amino acids held together by peptide bonds; a protein can be distinguished from fats and carbohydrates by the presence of nitrogen.

- **Amino acids:** The building blocks of proteins; an amino acid falls into one of four categories: nonpolar (valine, glycine), polar (serine, tyrosine), acidic (aspartic acid, glutamic acid), and basic (histidine, lysine).

- **Lipids:** Fatty acids in which energy is stored. Examples include waxes, oils, and cholesterol.

Key laboratory techniques

- **Extraction:** A technique in which a solute is distributed between two substances of different polarities, such as oil and water.

- **Chromatography:** The separation of a mixture by passing it through one of several materials that absorb some of its compounds. The result is usually that the various components of the mixture are distributed in distinct layers. Types of chromatography include gas-liquid, paper, and thin-layer chromatography.

- **Distillation:** The process by which liquids are separated based on their boiling points. When a liquid is boiled, for instance, the substance with the lower boiling point evaporates, leaving only the substance with the higher boiling point. This is simple distillation. More advanced techniques include fractional and vacuum distillation.

- **Crystallization:** A separation technique in which a pure substance crystallizes, leaving an impure substance behind.

Biological Sciences Practice Exercises

Passage I (Questions 1–4)

The hypothalamic-pituitary-thyroid system develops in the fetus independently of the mother. The trapping of iodine occurs by 12 weeks' gestation, at which point the pituitary secretion of thyrotropin, or thyroid-stimulating hormone (TSH) begins. The primary function of the thyroid is the synthesis of thyroxine (T_4) and triiodothyronine (T_3).

Congenital hypothyroidism in infants can stunt the normal growth and development of a child unless the clinical progression of the disease is reversed by the administration of thyroid hormone to supplement or replace endogenous production. Pediatric doses of levothyroxine are as follows:

- Neonate to 6 months: 25–50 mcg/d
- 6–12 months: 50–75 mcg/d
- 1–6 years: 75–100 mcg/d
- 6–12 years: 100–150 mcg/d
- More than 12 years: 150 mcg/d

The delay of hypothalamic-pituitary axis re-adaptation may postpone the achievement of appropriate TSH levels for several months after the introduction of daily synthetic thyroxine. Hypothyroidism can be difficult to detect in its early stage, because in the short term, the body will prompt a failing thyroid gland to produce more hormones. Cold intolerance, puffiness, and coarse skin appear to occur far more rarely in younger patients than in older ones, while other more-common symptoms are difficult to detect in some children.

Hypothyroidism is classified as primary when the thyroid does not produce sufficient hormones; it is considered secondary when the pituitary does not produce sufficient thyroid stimulation hormone (TSH). Some medications have been associated with primary hypothyroidism, including amiodarone, interferon alpha, thalidomide, and lithium.

Congenital hypothyroidism is a comparatively rare form of the disease. In areas of adequate iodine intake, the most common form of hypothyroidism is autoimmune thyroiditis (Hashimoto thyroiditis). This causes the body to see thyroid antigens as foreign substances, causing a chronic immune reaction. Lymphonic infiltration of the thyroid and progressive destruction of thyroid tissue ensue. Antimicrosmal or antithyroid peroxidase (anti-TPO) antibodies are found more commonly than antithyroglobulin antibodies.

1. **Hypothyroidism is classified as tertiary when:**

    A. It is caused by inadequate production of thyrotropin-releasing hormone (TRH) by the hypothalamus.

    B. The hypothalamic-pituitary axis matures at a retarded rate, delaying the synthesis of TSH.

    C. Iodine deficiency prevents the thyroid from producing adequate T_3 and T_4 for child development.

    D. It is caused by lymphonic infiltration of the thyroid.

2. The presence of elevated TSH levels in a patient likely indicates which of the following:

I. *Overproduction of T_3*
II. *Underproduction of T_4*
III. *Hypothyroidism*
IV. *Hyperthyroidism*

A. I only.
B. I and III only.
C. II and III only.
D. II and IV only.

3. A 5-year-old has taken 75 mcg of levothyroxine daily for more than a year. The level of free T_4 in his blood has remained at the low end of the reference range. He has begun to report constipation but has shown no signs of excitability or nervousness. Which of the following is likely appropriate?

A. Dosage of 100 mcg levothyroxine daily.
B. Dosage of 50 mcg levothyroxine daily.
C. Daily iodine supplements.
D. Thalidomide.

4. Which of the following statements about the hypothalamic-pituitary axis is NOT true?

A. It could accurately be described as the coordination of hormone production between the brain and various glands, including the thyroid, via the pituitary.

B. It will inhibit the regulation of thyroid hormone via synthetic means by mediating the production of thyroxine.

C. When given signals by the hypothalamus to stimulate TSH production, the pituitary releases T_3 and T_4 hormones.

D. It can trigger hormonal changes in response to external cues such as light and temperature.

5. **Diisobutylaluminium hydride (DIBAH) is a reducing agent that is useful in converting esters to aldehydes. Which of the following elements is DIBAH likely to contain in the greatest quantity?**

A. Oxygen.
B. Carbon.
C. Nitrogen.
D. Hydrogen.

6. **A solvent mixture is drawn up a thin sheet of glass coated with silica gel using a capillary tube, resulting in a distribution of analytes on the glass. Which of the following laboratory techniques has been utilized?**

A. Distillation.
B. Oxidation.
C. Chromatography.
D. Halogenation.

conclusion

You have made it through all 101 tips, the dozens (and dozens) of formulas, and all the information and advice wedged in between. Feel like you know it all now? Do not be surprised if you do not, because we should face the facts: Tests like the MCAT are designed to test your ability to make sense of new situations, not the ones you have already seen.

Still, if you have mastered the concepts in this book and practiced on actual MCAT questions through a number of — and we mean many, many — practice tests, you should feel prepared. And feeling prepared should also cut down on the anxiety and stress that accompany any hurdle that waits between you and your plans for your future.

When it is all over, think back on your time studying for the MCAT as good preparation for what came after: the demands of medical school; the uncertainty of practicing medicine; the long hours of hard, sometimes solitary work that all doctors put into their jobs. But most of all, when it is all over, do not think too much of it. Your future awaits.

appendix  A

Internet Resources

Overall MCAT preparation and information

Association of American Medical Colleges (www.aamc.org): The official site for the MCAT. This should be your first stop to do the official practice test, review information about the test, and sign up to take it. The AAMC also sells practice tests.

MCAT Review (http://mcat-review.org): This is a fairly comprehensive and free Web site created by students who have an ongoing project in which test takers submit their best tips in an effort to "crack the MCAT."

Test Prep Review (www.testprepreview.com): This site will try to sell you its books and courses, but it also has some useful free practice. Try the self-assessment quizzes in dozens of topics. Also, follow the "Self Improvement Directory" link to find lists of free resources in a variety of subject areas.

Princeton Review (www.princetonreview.com): Princeton Review sells test preparation books and courses on the MCAT, and its Web site also has some free resources once you sign in. If you feel you need to take a course or purchase more study materials, this is one of several good sources for those resources.

Kaplan (www.kaplan.com): Another prominent and test-preparation company, Kaplan offers some free content on its Web site in addition to information about its courses and other products.

ExamKrackers (www.examkrackers.com): Another test preparation company whose materials are generally for sale only, ExamKrackers sells comprehensive content guides to all MCAT subjects. These could be a good buy if you need a lot of help learning (or remembering) physics, chemistry, or biology concepts, but do not want to take a full course.

MCATPrep.net (www.mcatprep.net): This site will try to sell you a book, but it also offers free practice tests and a free list of MCAT formulas.

Science resources

MCAT 45 (www.mcat45.com): This free site was in the process of posting a complete study guide to the science portions of the MCAT at the time of publication. It also has a blog and forum on the test, and offers online tutoring.

Biology Online (www.biology-online.org): A good site for general information on biology concepts.

TheFreeDictionary (http://medical-dictionary.thefreedictionary.com): This free online dictionary is a good place to quickly look up a word whose meaning has escaped you, particularly for the biology section of the test.

Math resources

Math.com (www.math.com): This site offers free tutorials and practice sets broken down by topic and concept. While this is not specifically geared toward the MCAT, it is a great place to catch up in your weak math areas.

The Math Forum (http://mathforum.org): This site is a clearinghouse for helpful information on all types of math problems. There is some paid content, but many of the links are free. Try clicking on "Internet Math Library" to search by concept.

Writing resources

EssayInstitute (www.essayinstitute.com): If you click on the "Writing Resources" tab here, you will find a brief, helpful checklist of grammatical issues to consider as you write. This company also offers paid grading of practice essays.

The online version of the Princeton Review has the MCAT Essay LiveGrader at **www.princetonreview.com/medical/mcat-essay-livegrader. aspx**, a service that provides specific, professional feedback on your essays that is tailored to the MCAT. This can help you get a better idea of your individual strengths and weaknesses, though it will probably not be necessary unless your writing skills are poor, or you are determined to gain an especially good score.

For a list of writing sample prompts that have appeared on the MCAT, try the AAMC site: **www.aamc.org/students/mcat/preparing/writing-sampleitems.htm**.

appendix B

*Physical Sciences
Answer Explanations*

1. If a motorboat travels 5 knots per hour west for three hours, but the wind pushes it back at 3 knots per hour, how far does the boat go?

   A. 5 knots.

   B. 6 knots.

   C. 3 knots.

   D. 0 knots.

To solve this, you would need to use the equation for displacement, as the position of the boat is changing: $d = \frac{1}{2}(v_o + v_f)t$. You are solving for displacement (d), and the two velocities are 5 and 3 knots. You would plug the 3 in to the equation as negative (-3), because the wind is going in the opposite direction of the boat. The time is 3 hours. Therefore, your calculation would look like this:

$d = \frac{1}{2} (5 + -3)3$

$d = \frac{1}{2} (2)3$

$d = \frac{1}{2}(6)$

$d = 3$ knots

✔ The correct answer is **(C)**.

2. **Electricity is created by placing zinc and copper solutions in two half-cells connected by a salt bridge. Which of the following is NOT true?**

   A. The electricity is produced by a galvanic cell.

   B. The electricity is produced by a voltaic cell.

   C. The electrical energy is produced by the movement of electrons.

   D. The salt bridge is used to draw extraneous molecules from the reaction, creating a greater electrical output.

Answer choices **(A)** and **(B)** and **(C)** are all accurate because the question describes a galvanic cell, also called a voltaic cell, in which the movement of electrons between two electrically conducting chemical phases is the basis of a galvanic cell. The role of the salt bridge in this process, however, is mischaracterized. The purpose of the salt bridge is to create a liquid bridge between the two solutions while minimizing the transfer of ions across the junction.

✔ Because **(D)** is the inaccurate statement, it is the correct answer.

3. **A child is riding on an amusement park ride. She sits in a seat that swings around a central pole on a chain. Which of the following would represent how fast she is moving?**

   A. The square root of [(the force pulling her toward the center pole times the distance from her to the pole)/the combined mass of the girl and her swing].

B. (The force pulling her away from the center pole/the force pulling her toward the center pole) times the combined mass of the girl and her swing.

C. The square root of [(the force pulling her away from the center pole times the distance from her to the pole)/the combined mass of the girl and her swing].

D. The square root of (the force pulling her toward the center pole/the mass of the girl and her swing).

This problem would use the formula for centripetal force: $F_c = (mv^2)/r$. We are asked to solve this for the velocity (v). If we manipulate the equation, we would find that $v^2 = F_c r/m$ and $v = \sqrt{F_c r/m}$. Now we must consider what the other variables stand for in this scenario. F_c, or centripetal force, is the force exerted by the rope, which is pulling the girl and the swing toward the center pole. Mass would refer to the combined mass of the girl and the swing, which are both being pulled constantly pulled toward the center. The radius (r) of the circle being created as the swing goes around the pole would be the distance between the center and the swing.

To recap:

F_c = the force pulling the girl toward the center pole

m = the mass of the girl and her swing

r = the distance between the girl (or the swing) and the pole

$v = \sqrt{F_c r/m}$

Note that choice (C) would be appealing if you misunderstood how centripetal force works; the force involved pulls toward the center of the circle, not away from it. Therefore, her speed is equal to the square root of [(the force pulling her toward the center pole times the distance from her to the pole)/the combined mass of the girl and her swing].

✔ The answer is **(A)**.

4. **Which of the following is true of the sound waves emitted by a racecar as it approaches the point on the track closest to your seat at the racetrack?**

I. *Their frequency, as observed by you, is higher than the frequency of the waves emitted by the car.*

II. *Their wavelength, as observed by you, is higher than the wavelength emitted by the car.*

III. *They make the sound you hear higher-pitched than the sound the car is actually making.*

IV. *They would make the sound you hear higher-pitched than it would otherwise be only if you were walking toward the track.*

A. I and III only.

B. I and IV only.

C. I, II, and III only.

D. I, II, and IV only.

This question is based on the Doppler effect, which in its simplest form states that the frequency of a wave will change based on the positions of the source of the wave and the observer. As the source of a sound approaches the observer, the frequency of the waves relative to the observer is higher; therefore, the sound the observer hears is higher-pitched. So Roman numerals I and III are true in this situation. As the car approaches your seat, the frequency of the waves as observed by you will rise, creating a higher-pitched sound.

Frequency is inversely proportional to wavelength, however, so Roman number II would not be true; the wavelength, as observed by you, would decrease relative to the actual wavelength. Roman numeral IV is a bit trickier, adding relative velocity to the picture. However, because the car is moving much faster than you are, your movement toward the car does not change the direction of the relative velocity. If you were moving toward the car at a faster speed, however, you would hear the sound of the car at a lower pitch.

✔ The answer is (**A**).

5. **The partial pressure of atmospheric oxygen gas at sea level is 160 mm Hg. If the oxygen makes up 21 percent of all atmospheric gases, which of the following is NOT true of hydrogen, which makes up 78 percent of the atmosphere?**

    A. Its partial pressure is roughly 600 mm Hg.

    B. The pressure exerted by hydrogen is greater than the pressure exerted by an ideal gas.

    C. Ozone makes up less than 1 percent of atmospheric gases.

    D. The pressure exerted by the atmosphere is greater than 700 mm Hg.

As with other negation questions, you will have to evaluate the accuracy of each answer choice in order to find which one is not true. With some simple calculation, you can find that the partial pressure of hydrogen is indeed 600 mm Hg, so answer choice (**A**) is correct. Knowing that Dalton's law states that all of the partial pressures of a mixed gas add up to the total pressure, this can be done as a simple proportion. If 160 mm Hg is exerted by 21 percent of the gas, then the total pressure of the atmosphere is about 760 mm Hg; 78 percent of that is about 600 mm Hg. In doing these calculations, we also find that **(D)** is correct.

However, **(B)** is not correct because a real gas will always exert less pressure than an ideal gas. Even though we are pretty sure we have found the inaccurate answer choice, we should still check answer choice **(C)**. Because oxygen and hydrogen make up 99 percent of atmospheric gases, and we know there are gases other than those two and ozone in the atmosphere, ozone must make up less than 1 percent of atmospheric gases.

✔ Because **(B)** is the inaccurate answer choice, it is the correct answer to this negation problem.

6. **A man jumps off of a bridge with a bungee attached to his foot, and his head just touches the water before he bounces back up. Which of the following statements is true?**

   A. The greater the elasticity of the bungee, the greater the force pulling the man toward the water.

   B. The longer the bungee, the greater the force pushing the man back toward the bridge.

   C. The greater the difference between the normal length and its length when the man hits the water, the greater the force pushing the man back toward the bridge.

   D. Hooke's law will apply once the bungee has reached the elastic limit.

Answer choice **(A)** is a bit backward. A more elastic bungee would allow the man to fall farther, but not because of a greater force pulling him toward the water; his weight and gravity are pulling him down, and neither of those have changed. He would fall farther because there would be less force pulling him back toward the bridge as he fell. Answer choice **(B)** has fallen short of encapsulating Hooke's law by saying the length of the bungee is proportional to the force exerted by the bungee as it returns to its normal length. Hooke's law ($F = -kx$) is accurately articulated in answer choice **(C)**, the correct answer. The force exerted by the bungee as it returns to its normal shape is directly proportional to the difference between the normal length of the bungee and its length at full extension. That difference is represented by the variable x, and k is a constant; the negative sign is present only because the force is being exerted in the opposite direction. Answer choice **(D)** also mischaracterizes Hooke's law. The law applies *until* the force exceeds the modulus of elasticity, not once that threshold is reached.

✔ The correct answer is **(C)**.

appendix C

Verbal Reasoning
Answer Explanations

1. **According to this article, what is the main reason why NASA has not gone farther into space?**

   A. The American public gets bored easily.
   B. NASA does not have enough competition.
   C. NASA is a government bureaucracy that avoids risks.
   D. There have been too many tragedies in the space program.

This is a main idea question, though it is a bit confusing because it is somewhat disguised as a question about a specific argument or detail. Keep in mind that the first question after the passage is nearly always a main idea question; this should help you steer clear of some problems. In this question, the overall argument being made in the passage is that space exploration should be left to private companies rather than the federal government, and the correct answer, **(C)**, captures that idea. His main contention is that NASA has not proceeded farther into space because it is risk-aversive due to being a government bureaucracy; therefore, space exploration should be left up to private companies. Several of the other answer choices include arguments and ideas that were stated in the passage but are not consistent with this main idea.

Answer choice **(A)** is a sentiment expressed by the author about the American public, but it is not the main reason that the author gives for why NASA has not gone farther into space. Answer choice **(B)** is even more tempting, because the author discusses the possibility that NASA needs more competition in the context of discussing NASA's one great success (the race for the Moon) and why NASA was successful (America was competing with another country, the Soviet Union). He does not put this forward as an ideal solution because his intended solution — and the main idea of the passage — is that private enterprise should take over space travel. **(D)** may be a consequence of NASA's attitude but is also a subjective criterion; how many deaths are too many? Also, the tolerance of risk in NASA has fluctuated over the years and was much higher when NASA was competing with the Soviet Union.

2. **What does the author believe we should do in the future to further the cause of space travel?**

    A. Get rid of NASA.
    B. Increase private enterprise in space travel.
    C. Get into a competition with another country.
    D. Only do big programs like the Apollo program from now on.

This is another main idea question, and the answer is **(B)**. From the very first paragraph, the author argues that people in the private sector have created the most significant innovations. However, he does not propose that we phase out government agencies like NASA, since they have worked in the past (the Apollo program), when governments have competed with each other. Therefore, **(A)** is incorrect. He mentions China as a possible competitor in the future but expresses the concern that other governments are not always available to spur competition. Therefore, **(C)** is not correct, either. Though he does mention NASA's overly strong focus on low earth orbit programs like the space shuttle, his examples of private enterprise programs in space are also relatively non-flashy low earth orbit programs. You can then infer that this author does not believe **(D)**, either.

3. **Name one technological innovation that the author does NOT mention in the article.**

   A. The Macintosh computer.
   B. The car.
   C. The airplane.
   D. The space shuttle.

This is a negation question, and as such it should be answered using the process of elimination.

The first paragraph of the article mentions the Wright Brothers (who invented the airplane), and the creation of Apple (the maker of the Macintosh). Paragraph six discusses the tragedy of the Challenger space shuttle **(D)**. Thus, **(A)**, **(C)**, and **(D)** are all mentioned in the article, and the answer is **(B)**.

The most effective way to answer this type of question is by process of elimination, but it can be slow. In this case, you may have gotten to the correct answer using association, instead. The article is about innovations and inventions in space travel. The computer, the airplane, and the Space Shuttle are all inventions related to or used in space travel. The car is not. Thus, the only innovation that is not related to space travel is the car, and the author is unlikely to have used that as an example in his article.

4. **According to the author, what was the main problem that caused the Challenger crash?**

   I. *A faulty O-ring.*

II. *A lack of communication between the company and NASA.*

III. *An overly complex bureaucracy.*

IV. *Government interference.*

A. Only I is correct.

B. Only II and IV are correct.

C. Only I, II, and IV are correct.

D. Only I, II, and III are correct.

To complete this Roman numeral problem, you should take each statement individually, keeping track of which ones are true according to the passage. This is also a retrieval problem that asks you to refer to a specific part of the passage. If you have made good annotations and highlights, you should be able to quickly find that the answer is **(D)**. In the article, the author blames the Challenger crash on a faulty O-ring (a fault in manufacturing), a lack of communication between the company that made the O-ring and NASA, and NASA's overly complex bureaucracy. He does not mention government interference, whether or not it occurred.

This one is tricky because **(C)** and **(D)** include the two variations on the theme of bureaucracy and government that the author frequently brings up in his article. Here, you want to use the one that adheres most closely to the article. Remember, though, that a retrieval question is going to refer to a specific part of the passage, and may not encompass the overall theme. So, in these cases, if you are in a hurry, keep in mind that the more precise version is usually the answer. "Government interference" is quite vague and can mean many things." An overly complex bureaucracy" is not especially precise, but is more so than "government interference," and is much closer to what the author discusses in his paragraph on the Challenger crash.

5. **What is author saying about Burt Rutan when he says, "Burt Rutan has said that he has never worked a day in his life."?**

   A. Burt Rutan has a poor work ethic.
   B. Burt Rutan has never held a regular job.
   C. Burt Rutan is very committed to the idea of space travel.
   D. Burt Rutan does not expect to get paid for his work.

This is an inference question in which you must restate what the author meant in the given statement. In context with the rest of the paragraph, the author is trying to say that Burt Rutan really loves his work on space travel, not that he is lazy **(A)**, which could also be considered extreme language, or perpetually unemployed **(B)**. Whether he expects to get paid **(D)** is not mentioned, so it would fall outside the parameter of the passage. The answer is **(C)**.

Watch out for metaphors and other word play. The important thing here is context. Alone, this sentence might seem to indicate that Burt Rutan does not work, but in context with the rest of the article, this is clearly an exaggeration to show how much he loves his work on his innovations related to space travel. With this type of question, keep the author's main idea in mind. Many ideas will pop up, especially in longer articles, but you should always look at them through the lens of the main idea. All arguments and examples in the article are intended to support its main point.

6. **What does the author mean by the term "space tourism"?**

   A. Visits by civilians to NASA-run facilities, such as the International Space Station.
   B. Trips to the moon.
   C. Visits to the Smithsonian National Air and Space Museum.
   D. Round trips in low earth orbit vehicles.

"Space tourism," though it sounds vague, is a specific term used by those promoting private industry in space exploration. In the context of the article, you can rather easily determine that the author does not mean visits to museums on earth (C) or the involvement of civilians in government agencies (A). You can also infer from the author's examples of private industry that he is not projecting very far into the future, and that his main interest in this area lies in activities set immediately around the earth. Space tourism to the moon is very much a thing of the not-near future. The correct answer is (D).

When answering definition questions, whether of a word or of a phrase, always remember that you are answering them within the context of the question and article. This holds true of questions in other sections, as well. This article, for example, is not speaking in terms of science fiction, but in terms of things that could be done today or within the next five or ten years, depending on whether there was demand for this kind of tourism and a company able to supply it. It is also discussing technological issues. These two parameters immediately cut out answers involving museums or the moon. The author's focus on private enterprise clues you in that any answer involving NASA is also incorrect. Knowing the general tone and intent of the article will help you answer this type of question quickly. Try to avoid having to hunt for the term and concentrate on its place in the article, instead.

appendix *D*

Writing Sample Responses

Prompt 1: Civil Disobedience

Civil disobedience is the best response to unfair laws.

Write an essay in which you do the following: Explain the meaning of the above statement. Describe a specific instance when civil disobedience is not the best response to unfair laws. Discuss what you think determines when civil disobedience is an appropriate/inappropriate response.

Low score

I do not agree with civil disobedience and think that it is bad. People who engage in civil disobedience have no respect for the government and just want what they want. They are always whining about how the government does things that they do not like. Meanwhile, people in our armed services are fighting overseas for the freedoms that these people back home abuse. They should not be allowed to disrespect the true patriots who are giving up their lives for our freedoms.

Our Founding Fathers fought hard to ensure that we had a free and prosperous life. They dumped British tea overboard during the Boston Tea Party to protest the unfair taxes of colonial government. That could have gotten them killed. It even did get some of them killed when they fought during the Revolutionary War. Later, Union soldiers died in the Civil War, which was fought to end slavery and make everybody free and equal. So, I do not think that people should engage in civil disobedience and disrespect our forefathers and soldiers like that.

Analysis

This essay suffers from a number of problems. First and foremost, it does not address the prompt. The prompt is not about whether or not civil disobedience is good or bad, but whether it is the best response to unfair laws. The essay also fails to define the prompt, which leads to numerous problems for the essay writer in later paragraphs. Always restate the prompt in your own words to establish for the grader that you understand the prompt and also to remind yourself what the prompt is about. If you do not restate the prompt in your own words, then you risk not thinking about it in sufficient depth to avoid making errors such as the essay writer makes above.

Notably, the essay writer contradicts him/herself by stating that civil disobedience is "bad" and that "people who engage in civil disobedience have no respect for the government and just want what they want," while one of the three examples that the writer gives (the Boston Tea Party) clashes with this position. The Boston Tea Party is a famous historical incident in which American colonists engaged in civil disobedience in their fight for independence.

Another example, the Union soldiers who fought and died in the Civil War, suffers from oversimplification of the war's causes (the war was more of a dispute over states' rights, with slavery only one of several grievances) and results (the war ended slavery in the United States but did not make every American "free and equal"). However, the main problem with the example is that it contradicts the writer's points by supporting the original statement of the prompt. The writer ignores the fact that many Americans practiced civil disobedience, both before and during the Civil War, in protest against the institution of slavery, even though slavery was legal in both the North and the South until the Emancipation Proclamations of 1862 and 1863.

As for the third example, while it does not directly contradict the writer's thesis, it does not support the writer's thesis, either. The writer states that those who practice civil disobedience show disrespect toward soldiers who fight and die in American wars, but the writer gives no evidence to support this. Without evidence, it is an opinion, not an argument. This argument is also an emotional one, which lowers the tone of the essay. Try to avoid these. You should maintain an objective distance from your subject and avoid formulating hostile arguments or personal attacks. While the writer's grammar is not poor, the essay's style is informal. The writer frequently uses contractions, as well as the first person point of view. Using a contraction here or there is not likely to harm the tone of your essay, but using contractions so often coupled with the use of first person point of view makes the tone of the essay too informal.

Finally, this essay is far too short. There is no set length for your essay; however, the parameters of the assignment and time limit generally constrain it to be a standard 500–800-word length. This essay, which is less than 200 words, is far too short to comprehensively address the prompt. The essay is also too short in its number of paragraphs. Again, there is no actual limit on how many paragraphs you write, but it is much easier to separate the three major tasks of your essay into three paragraphs than to attempt to compact them into two paragraphs. As this essay shows, having only two paragraphs makes it too easy to leave out important points and allow the essay to become disorganized. This is why you should separate your tasks into three paragraphs.

Average score

Civil disobedience has a long and respected history in the United States. Many of our founding fathers practiced civil disobedience in their fight against the British during the American Revolution. Abolitionists practiced civil disobedience in opposing slavery before the Civil War. Civil rights activists practiced civil disobedience in protest again segregation in the South during the 1950s and 1960s. Anti-war activists demonstrated against the Vietnam War in the 1960s and 1970s. Civil disobedience is embedded in the very fabric of American society.

Yet, civil disobedience has its down sides. It has been used to resist social change (as when protesters against desegregation of schools demonstrated against the busing of students to distant schools to integrate them racially). It has been used by antigovernment protesters who used violent means to resist laws that they did not like. These could range from taxes (Ruby Ridge) to endangerment and sexual abuse of children (the siege at Waco). Civil disobedience is not always a good or positive thing when the resistance is violent and/or the laws are not unfair.

Civil disobedience is a tradition that has both a light and a dark side. It has helped to advance civil liberties and it has also served to hold them back. It all depends on the laws that are being upheld and challenged and, of course, people will not always agree on which laws are good and which are bad. Yet civil disobedience is extremely important to the history and current political health of the United States. It is part of our nation's history and something in which we should all be proud.

Analysis

This essay has some improvements on the low-scored essay. For a start, it clearly addresses the topic of civil disobedience and gives several examples of it. The writer also gives an antithesis that shows how civil disobedience is not always progressive but can be reactionary as well. The writer acknowledges that civil disobedience has a dark side while insisting that it is still a necessary tool in the democratic process. However, there are some problems with the essay. First and foremost, the writer fails to answer the prompt, which states that civil disobedience is the *best* response to unfair laws. The writer also fails to define civil disobedience, which makes it difficult for the writer to formulate a response to the antithesis.

In his discussion of the dark side of civil disobedience, the writer puts several examples in parentheses without fully explaining what happened during these incidents and why they are examples of civil disobedience gone awry. In the final paragraph, the writer does not develop his stance on when civil disobediences is the best response to unfair laws. He simply says that it is sometimes an appropriate response, which does not fulfill the task he was given. In addition, this essay is only about 300 words — still too short to allow its writer to fully develop his ideas. Therefore, the writer does not quite do the job necessary to write a successful essay.

High score

Civil disobedience is a highly controversial part of American politics and is embedded in the very fabric of American culture. Many famous Americans, from Paul Revere to Martin Luther King Jr., have used it to bring about change. Civil disobedience is the breaking of an unjust law in order to show its injustice and bring about a change in the legal system to more equality and fairness. Civil disobedience occurs when other avenues have been exhausted. It is the best and most effective way to undo an unjust law.

Civil disobedience has existed since the period of Colonial America. The Pilgrims came over in 1620 to escape religious persecution and practice their own religion in a new society. Their descendants dumped tea into the Boston Harbor during the Revolutionary War to protest unfair taxation. Abolitionists before and during the Civil War fought slavery (sometimes, like John Brown, violently), staging protests and setting up the Underground Railroad. This was a network of safe houses for runaway slaves that conveyed them north to Canada and freedom. African-American civil rights workers defied unfair segregation laws by sitting at lunch counters reserved for white people. Vietnam War protesters threw demonstrations where they burned draft cards and American flags to protest what they saw as an unjust war that was killing American soldiers in the tens of thousands. All of these groups brought about necessary change, even though it was not popular enough to be pushed through politically at the time, through the publicity and example that civil disobedience generated.

But there is a dark side to civil disobedience, as well. It can be used to resist change and also to bully the majority into obeying what a violent minority wants. Nineteenth-century British weavers protesting the introduction of new industrial looms broke those machines in protest. This earned them the name of "luddites," since used for anyone who has a kneejerk reaction to technological progress. The Ku Klux Klan terrorized anyone in the South who supported desegregation and equality of African-Americans after the Civil War in the 1870s, 1920s, and again in the 1950s. Antigovernment individuals and groups like those who destroyed their own compound at Waco, or perpetrated the Oklahoma City bombing in 1995, or bombed abortion clinics in the 1980s and 1990s have tried to impose their own ideas about freedom and nongovernmental interference on others through fear.

This does not change the fact that civil disobedience is the best way to tear down unjust laws. Unjust laws are pushed through by the majority, but that does not make them correct. It does, however, make them very difficult to change legally. How do you change a law when it is precisely what most people want the law to be? It is like the film, *Inherit the Wind,* based on the famous "Scopes Monkey Trial" from the 1920s in which a young teacher decides to defy the ban on teaching evolution as a form of civil disobedience. If he and people like him had not done so, scientific teaching in America would have been held back for decades, mired in pre-Darwinian thinking. Therefore, civil disobedience is the best way to deal with such laws. The very fact that it can be abused to take down just laws as well is only a testament to its power. It must certainly be used well and correctly, but against an unjust law, it is often the only true defense. This is why it has such a long tradition of use that continues to this day.

Analysis

This essay gets the highest score, not because it is perfect, but because it does its job. First, it restates the prompt. Second, it defines the primary term in the prompt, "civil disobedience," and gives detailed examples from history to illustrate that term and how it fits into the prompt. Third, the essay uses these examples both to support the writer's position in favor of the prompt's statement and to set up and refute the antithesis.

The essay also has an even, objective tone. The writer gives an opinion, but also supports this opinion with evidence. Positive and negative examples of civil disobedience are provided and also evaluated for their similarities and differences. For example, the writer distinguishes the negative examples as attempts by some individuals and groups to bully the general population into going their way through violence and intimidation rather than peaceful resistance and demonstration by example. It is this example that shows the essay's final strength — the writer refutes the antithesis by showing that the very fact that civil disobedience can be dangerous shows its power to overturn unjust laws that are too popular to be repealed by legal means.

Thus, the writer uses the very strength of the antithesis in favor of the prompt and the essay's thesis. Recruiting the antithesis and turning it to your favor is one of the most effective ways of refuting it, often more effective than simply attacking it or otherwise directly opposing it.

You may also have noticed that this essay is broken down into more than three paragraphs. This is acceptable, as the content would still be in the order of the tasks given, though you can write a solid essay in three paragraphs that addresses the three main issues of the assignment. However, you may also feel it necessary to write more than three paragraphs. If that works for you, do it. The three-paragraph format is intended as a guideline to help you better organize your essay.

Prompt 2: Abortion

Abortion is a woman's right to choose.

Write an essay in which you do the following: Explain the meaning of the above statement. Describe a specific instance where abortion should not be a choice. Discuss whether abortion is a woman's right to choose.

Low score

(Spelling and grammar have not been changed.)

Since time began, women have had to put up with men making decisions about what they should do with their bodies, telling them what to do all the time and hurting them. It needs to stop. Woman should be able to make their own decisions and not rely on some man to make them for her. It is her body, not yours, boys!

There are some who say that abortion is bad because it kills the fetus. But that only works if the fetus is a real person before it is born and we do not know if that is really true or not. It is just another excuse to try to force women to cede control over there own bodies to men. That is just not fair to women. Women should have the right to choose what to do with their bodies. After all, we all know that they will be the ones who are forced to raise the child if they give birth to it.

Abortion is a highly controversial topic that has divided America for many years. It makes a lot of people angry and it should not. It should just be a given that women have the right to do what they want with their own bodies.

Analysis

The three main problems with this essay are the tone, a repetitious argument, and a lack of evidence. First is the tone, which is highly argumentative. The essay writer comes across as hostile and defensive, attacking men in general for trying to control women. Though the writer does address the prompt to a certain extent, he/she does so in a polemical and extremely one-sided way that quickly leaves behind the prompt in favor of the writer's own intent.

The essay writer also repeats the same argument instead of presenting more than one. This also means that the writer's middle task — addressing the antithesis — is perfunctory. No sooner does the writer present the antithesis, but he/she immediately returns to the same point made in the previous paragraph without refuting the antithesis in any substantive way.

These two problems lead to the third, which is that the essay writer presents little or no evidence to support his/her thesis that abortion is an issue only because men are trying to take control of women's bodies from women. While the writer could argue this point because it is a restatement of sorts of the prompt, there is little or no actual supporting evidence, no discussion of Roe v. Wade or any of the decisions since then. While the author acknowledges that "abortion is a highly controversial topic that has divided America for many years", he or she still insists that it is a "given" that women should have the right to have abortions if they so choose and skirts the controversy by insisting that women have the right to do whatever they want with their bodies, even when pregnant.

The writer also uses vague terminology, such as beginning with the phrase, "Since time began" and "we all know." These are empty phrases that supply no new information to the reader and set up expectations that the writer cannot possibly fulfill within the parameters of the essay. There is no way to prove, for example, that a situation involving human behavior has occurred "since time began" or that "we all know" (the author and everyone in the audience) about an argument or piece of evidence. If everyone knows something, then it need not be argued in the first place and certainly is not controversial.

Finally, the writer makes several grammatical and stylistic errors in the essay itself. For example, "Woman should be able to make their own decisions and not rely on some man to make them for her" has an incorrect number for its subject "woman," which should be "women." Watch out for these simple errors. They can be easily made in the heat of writing an essay under the time restrictions.

Average score

Abortion is a highly controversial topic that has divided many Americans against each other. Ever since Roe vs. Wade came out in 1973, making abortion legal, people have been trying to overturn it again. The central issue is whether a woman should have control over her own body, even if it comes to terminating a fetus in the womb. Some argue that the fetus is a living child already and must be protected at all costs, even to the risk of the mother. Others argue that the fetus is not yet alive and cannot be considered as having more rights than the mother that carries it. Either way, the law states that a woman has a right to decide whether she wants to carry a fetus nine months to term or not, since she is the one who will be stuck with the responsibility and, in some cases, the danger of giving birth.

Abortion is not a completely unproblematical issue, however. For example, there is the issue of what to do about late-term abortions (usually six months or later). As medical science becomes increasingly able to save babies who are born prematurely, even as far back as six months, politicians and the public have become increasingly uneasy about aborting fetuses that are viable and could be born. Therefore, late-term abortions are illegal in most states.

Even so, abortion is ultimately the responsibility and choice of the mother. She is the one who must carry the child to term, and it is better for her health and the health of any babies that she might have in the future that she be allowed to choose whether she should carry a pregnancy to term. It is better for her to have an abortion than to have a baby that she does not want, especially if having a child would endanger her life. Even though abortion should probably have restrictions on it to prohibit terminations of viable fetuses, these restrictions should not violate the mother's rights to her own body. That last is an inalienable, constitutional right, as Roe vs. Wade recognized.

Analysis

This essay is overall decent in addressing the overall issue of abortion. It also more-or-less answers the prompt. However, it falls down in failing to restate the prompt in a clear and concise manner at the beginning of the essay and in not defining its main term "abortion." This gets the writer into some trouble during the antithesis paragraph when he or she struggles with why abortion in general is legal and approved by the public, but late-term abortions are illegal and not approved. How can the two be different? Here is where defining abortion and its limits would have helped.

The essay's examples of when abortion might be appropriate are also a little vague. The writer mentions Roe v. Wade but does not discuss or explain the court decision or its connection to the abortion issue. The essay mentions situations where a woman's right to have an abortion should be restricted, but does not get into much detail about why. The writer could get more points by refining the examples and more clearly connecting them to the prompt.

High score

The issue of abortion is intimately tied up with the right of a woman to choose what to do with her own body. Because only women can have babies and carry them to term for nine months, they are also the ones who should make the ultimate decision of whether or not to terminate their pregnancies with an abortion. While this is not a perfect solution, it is better than taking away the right of a woman to decide what to do with her own body or medical care. Allowing women the right to have an abortion is the lesser evil.

There are people who strenuously object to this right. Many religious groups, such as the Catholic church, believe that life begins at conception, not birth. So they feel that abortion is murder. These groups also often feel that women should defer to male authority figures in decisions about their bodies even as they elevate motherhood as the greatest (or only role) that a woman can have. Such groups point to certain practices such as the use of abortion as birth control and late-term abortions (where the fetus might be far along enough in development to survive outside the mother's body) as evidence that abortion is inherently evil and should not be legal.

The Supreme Court decision in Roe v. Wade in 1973, which made abortion legal in the United States, has therefore become a touchstone for such groups, who have since tried their hardest to overturn it.

But these groups ignore the fact that the idea that life begins at conception is not universal, and that even Roe v. Wade only made abortion legal up until the point that the fetus was viable (thus ruling out late-term abortions). These groups also have no answer for the studies that show the number of illnesses and deaths in women caused by botched abortions or dangerous pregnancies when abortion was illegal. A woman should not be forced to go through with a pregnancy that might kill her or have a child that she can in no way afford. Making abortion illegal does not stop women from having abortions because the lack of options that leads them to have abortions in the first place still exists.

Such groups also do not help their credibility by opposing options that give women more choices, such as increased availability of birth control, or by trying to intimidate women out of choosing abortion through aggressive and misleading counseling or picketing women's health clinics. While no one sees abortion as a wonderful thing, and it can cause women suffering afterward, having the choice also opens up other options for women, while eliminating it also eliminates those other options. Women should therefore have the right to seek an abortion as part of their overall control over their own bodies.

Analysis

This essay starts out by restating the prompt while also explaining why abortion is important to women. The essay writer asserts that abortion reflects women's general rights and control over their own bodies, thus explaining that this issue has to do with more than a single medical procedure. The writer then introduces the antithesis in the second paragraph.

The writer is careful to address the issues raised by groups opposed to abortion. This not only shows objectivity and respect for the opposing position to the prompt, but also makes it easier for the writer to explain in the following two paragraphs why the woman's right to control over her own body supersedes the objections of these groups. The problem with making fun of an opposing position, ignoring it or not properly explaining it, is that this makes it more difficult to formulate strong arguments to refute that position. As with this essay here, the writer should understand the opposing position to the prompt thoroughly before refuting it.

Prompt 3: Government Spending

A government should never spend more than it takes in.

Write an essay in which you do the following: Explain the meaning of the above statement. Describe a specific instance where a government should spend more than it takes in. Discuss whether a government should spend more than it takes in.

Low score

(Spelling and grammar have not been changed.)

If there is anything that this govenment crisis has taught us its that a govenment should never spend more than it takes in. U and I will end up paying for this mistakes for many years to come. It isn't reassuring when the President wants us to pay more and more money to fix already expensive mistakes. Where will it end? When should we say stop?

The govenment says that it needs the money for programs for the poor. Well, I do not see how that money ever gets to the poor, or the deserving poor, anyway, and how does that help the rest of us? If u really think that the government wants to help us, think again.

I think that the government should not be allowed to spend money and push up our debt until it breaks the bank and puts us into debt with foreign powers. then it will know whose boss.

Analysis

This essay suffers from a number of errors that lower its score. Although the essay writer does restate the prompt (albeit very literally) and does make a few good points (the reference to breaking the bank and putting the country in debt to foreign countries), the essay overall has numerous problems. First, it is too short. This is partly because the writer introduces a point then moves on with no argument or evidence. For example, the essay writer states that the government says that it gives money to the poor when it does not but provides no evidence to support this claim. All statements in an essay must be supported by argument and evidence, especially the refutation of the antithesis. Also, the second paragraph scarcely addresses the antithesis before disagreeing with it. The essay should devote more time to the antithesis than a brief statement and dismissal.

The essay also suffers from numerous spelling and grammar-error patterns. The essay writer persistently misspells "government," for example, and uses homonyms such as the possessive pronoun "its" instead of the grammatically correct contraction "it is." The writer also frequently uses text speak, writing "u" instead of "you." While graders are aware that you are writing under pressure and a time limit, it does not mean that error patterns in spelling and grammar cannot hurt you. Remember that the grader gives a grade based on his or her overall impression. Nothing hurts that impression like numerous grammar and spelling errors, particularly ones that show ignorance of a rule rather than a lapse here and there.

Average score

Everyone these days is thinking about the government and how it has changed from Bush to Obama. They want to know what the government will do for them to help them through the current economic crisis. But they are also worried about government spending. We have already spent a lot of money on the war in Iraq and other things and are really in debt. Obama wants us to spend even more to get ourselves out of debt, but this seems like just a way of making the problem worse. A lot of people think that we should start balancing the budget now and not later, that the government should stop spending more than it takes in.

Obama and his people say that this is the only way to get the country back on its feet. They want to tax the rich to help the poor, but that will take a while and they say we have to help the poor right now, not later. They also say that the middle class needs to be helped out and the gap between rich and poor closed. They say they want to help us and I believe them. I just wish I knew how they were going to do that. Nobody wants more taxes.

The government really needs to think more about this. Is a big spending bill the best way to help everybody out? Where will the money come from? Will it all come from the rich? What if they do not want to pay? What if the economy does not work? What if the foreign powers who lent us money want their money back? How will we pay them? Will they get control over our country? What is Obama doing?

I think that the government has a responsibility to tell us whatever is going on and keep us in the loop. We're entitled to that much after all the bad stuff that Bush put us through. And it would help if the government stopped the War already, too.

Analysis

The essay does restate the prompt in the first paragraph and does bring up the antithesis in paragraph two. However, it does not bring up the prompt until the end of the first paragraph. And while it discusses the antithesis, the essay does not refute it very clearly. The essay writer even seems willing to believe the antithesis as long as it is proved correct, yet goes on to argue for the prompt anyway. This is not a very good way of refuting the antithesis.

Another problem that arises is that while the third paragraph asks some good questions, it does not answer them. It also jumbles them all together in a disorganized group. When you ask a question in a paragraph, you should give your own answer to it before moving on to the next question or point.

Finally, the last paragraph returns to a statement from the first paragraph and discusses that. The problem with this is that the statement is not the prompt, which is what the essay should be discussing. Nor does the paragraph address the third task of the essay, to prove the prompt statement either true or false. Instead of giving the essay's final point about whether or not government should spend more than it takes in, the essay writer delivers a muddled and emotive point about government accountability. While the issue of accountability is certainly related to the issue of government spending, it is not the central issue of the prompt. You should end your essay with your position on the prompt, not a tangentially related issue.

High score

Government spending and accountability has been prominent in the minds of the American public recently. With the economy, by some estimates, doing worse than it has since the Great Depression of the 1930s, and a frightening national debt running into hundreds of billions of dollars, people want to know that the government is not spending their money unwisely. As such, the issue of whether the government should spend what it does not have comes up frequently. Should the government have a budget that exceeds what it takes in from taxes and other revenues? Many say no, that we are already in too deep, and that more spending will only dig us deeper.

The new government of President Barack Obama, however, disagrees. Having inherited a huge deficit from the previous presidential administration, Obama argues that the only way to bring the government back on track is to infuse the economy with much-needed cash and bail out the banks whose failure has exacerbated the economic crash, even though their incompetence helped precipitate that crash. Obama also insists that programs to help the poor and middle class must be put into place to alleviate needless suffering and to narrow the gap between rich and poor. Obama seeks to balance the budget to a certain extent by reversing many of his predecessor, George W. Bush's, tax cuts and increasing taxation of the wealthy. He also insists that by reviving the economy, we will also generate much of the necessary money that we need to repay our national debt. However, much of the money will need to come from loans by other countries like China. These loans will have to be paid back by the American people at some point and will put the deficit into trillions of dollars.

Also, the rich who have been doing well under the previous administration may not want to raise their taxes and contribute to the economic recovery. And the bailing out of the banks that went under may help the average American...or it might be throwing good money after bad. What if these banks go under again? What if the bailout only helps out the executives who got their banks into this mess in the first place? These are important considerations because the country is already in debt and does not have any extra money to throw around. Plus, a bail-out that only benefits rich corporate executives who did not do their job right does not stop, let alone redress, the growing imbalance between rich and poor.

That said, the Obama Administration has a point, one bolstered by its willingness to set a date for the end of the expensive war in Iraq that has been draining the American budget dry. Even if the action racks up more debt, we must do something. While balancing the budget so that the government spends no more than it takes in is an important ideal and laudable goal that would make America more solvent and independent of foreign influences, it does not seem like an achievable one right now. Or, more to the point, it does not seem achievable with the other, higher priorities currently on the table. Some experts have complained that the easy credit of the 1990s and early outs has allowed Americans to spend well past their financial limits. This may be true to a certain extent, but many Americans are struggling now to pay the rent or mortgage, not just pay for a nice, new, flat-screen television. Some have been struggling for much longer than last summer. They need help in keeping their homes and putting food on the table. It is not really their fault that food, rent, and gas prices have all shot up, raising living expenses in general. Therefore, while balancing the budget is a good goal for the future, right now the government should put this on the back burner and concentrate on getting the country out of its current economic crisis, first. Who knows? Once we revive the economy, we may even make that money back. We have done it before.

Analysis

This essay differs from the others in that it argues that the prompt is false, not true. It is not necessary to argue for a prompt in order to write a good essay. Here, the essay writer spends the latter part of the essay (the third task) to support the antithesis. Note that the essay writer does not leave the antithesis unchallenged. In fact, paragraphs two and three are devoted to both the antithesis and the arguments against it. But paragraphs four and five address these arguments and show why the essay writer agrees with the antithesis. Remember that you always have the option of arguing that the prompt is false, as well as true. The reason why most of the essays here argue for the prompt is because arguing that the prompt is true is usually easier than arguing that it is false. You can usually find more true reasons than false to put down when you brainstorm. However, if it is easier to argue that the prompt is false, you should do so.

The essay writer does something else that contributes heavily to the formal, objective, and authoritative tone of the essay. When discussing specific persons in the essay, especially those in positions of authority where they represent a group of people or institution, the writer gives that person's full name and title when first introducing the person. So, for example, the writer says "President Barack Obama" when first introducing him and only later refers to him as just "Obama." The writer also distinguishes between Barack Obama and the Obama Administration, which are two different, but related, entities.

This brings up a major issue that distinguishes between a poor or adequate essay and a good or excellent one: detail and precision of language. This essay has a great deal of detail and precision of language. Because the evaluation and grading of essays can be so holistic, it is easy to assume that this means that the grading criteria are also fuzzy and vague. Not so. You are expected to be as scientific in your approach to writing an essay as to filling out the multiple-choice questions in the science and verbal sections. The graders are aware that you are writing your two essays under time pressure and that you will not have access to extra material to research arguments and examples. However, by reading up on current events, you should have more than enough material at hand to write a good essay without recourse to extensive memorization or something more underhanded like cheating.

As such, you can write an essay like this one that is very precise in its language, introducing Obama and former President George W. Bush by their full names and titles, for example. Still, you have to approach detail with caution. You cannot just throw everything into the pot and hope that it boils. But you should make sure to put in all *necessary* detail. As with this essay, you should answer the usual basic questions of who, what, where, when, how, and why — especially how and why, in addition to the specific questions following the prompt. Until you have answered these questions, your argument remains incomplete.

appendix E

Biological Sciences
Answer Explanations

Passage I (Questions 1–4)

The hypothalamic-pituitary-thyroid system develops in the fetus independently of the mother. The trapping of iodine occurs by 12 weeks' gestation, at which point the pituitary secretion of thyrotropin, or thyroid-stimulating hormone (TSH), begins. The primary function of the thyroid is the synthesis of thyroxine (T_4) and triiodothyronine (T_3).

Congenital hypothyroidism in infants can stunt the normal growth and development of a child unless the clinical progression of the disease is reversed by the administration of thyroid hormone to supplement or replace endogenous production. Pediatric doses of levothyroxine are as follows:

- Neonate to 6 months: 25–50 mcg/d
- 6–12 months: 50–75 mcg/d
- 1–6 years: 75–100 mcg/d
- 6–12 years: 100–150 mcg/d
- More than 12 years: 150 mcg/d

The delay of hypothalamic-pituitary axis readaptation may postpone the achievement of appropriate TSH levels for several months after the introduction of daily synthetic thyroxine. Hypothyroidism can be difficult to detect in its early stages, because in the short term the body will prompt a failing thyroid gland to produce more hormones. Cold intolerance, puffiness, and coarse skin appear to occur far more rarely in younger patients than in older ones, while other more common symptoms are difficult to detect in some children.

Hypothyroidism is classified as primary when the thyroid does not produce sufficient hormones; it is considered secondary when the pituitary does not produce sufficient thyroid stimulation hormone (TSH). Some medications have been associated with primary hypothyroidism, including amiodarone, interferon alpha, thalidomide, and lithium.

Congenital hypothyroidism is a comparatively rare form of the disease. In areas of adequate iodine intake, the most common form of hypothyroidism is autoimmune thyroiditis (Hashimoto thyroiditis). This causes the body to see thyroid antigens as foreign substances, causing a chronic immune reaction. Lymphonic infiltration of the thyroid and progressive destruction of thyroid tissue ensue. Antimicrosmal or antithyroid peroxidase (anti-TPO) antibodies are found more commonly than antithyroglobulin antibodies. Worldwide, the most common cause of hypothyroidism.

1. **Hypothyroidism is classified as tertiary when:**

    A. It is caused by inadequate production of thyrotropin-releasing hormone (TRH) by the hypothalamus.

    B. The hypothalamic-pituitary axis matures at a retarded rate, delaying the synthesis of TSH.

C. Iodine deficiency prevents the thyroid from producing adequate T_3 and T_4 for child development.

D. It is caused by lymphonic infiltration of the thyroid.

This question is a good example of how biology passages are a lot like verbal reasoning passages: They are both full with lots of confusing and often unnecessary information. In this case, you need to recognize that the meaning of "tertiary" is related to "primary" and "secondary." Like any verbal reasoning question, we then need to re-read this part of the text, which states:

Hypothyroidism is classified as primary when the thyroid itself fails to produce sufficient thyroid hormones; it is considered secondary when the pituitary fails to produce sufficient thyroid stimulation hormone (TSH).

From here, we must gather all the clues we can. We should know from memorizing information on the endocrine system a bit about hypothyroidism — namely that it results from the under-production of hormones by the thyroid — but much of this passage is likely new information. We do, however, know that the production of hormones by the thyroid, pituitary, and other glands is a delicate balance in which the hormones produced in one gland affect the production of other hormones. From here, we could see that if problems in the pituitary cause the secondary form of the disease, the source of the tertiary form of the disease should be another step removed from the pituitary. We should also know that the area of the brain ultimately responsible for this dance is the hypothalamus. We also see in the passage a mention of the "hypothalamic-pituitary-thyroid system." Put these clues together, and we should recognize that (**A**) is the correct answer.

Answer choice (**B**) hints at the hypothalamic-pituitary connection but is incorrect because hypothyroidism does not result from a delay in production, but rather insufficient production of TSH and thyroid hormones.

The other answer choices refer to two causes of the disease, which is not what the question is asking.

✔ The answer is (**A**).

2. **The presence of elevated TSH levels in a patient likely indicates which of the following:**

   I.   *Over production of T_3*
   II. *Under production of T_4*
   III. *Hypothyroidism*
   IV. *Hyperthyroidism*

   A. I only.
   B. I and III only.
   C. II and III only.
   D. II and IV only.

It is clear from the passage — if not from prior knowledge — that hypothyroidism is caused by underproduction of thyroid hormones, while hyperthyroidism would be the reverse. To answer this question, then you need only to figure out whether elevated TSH levels would be associated with over-production or under-production of the two thyroid hormones, T_3 and T_4. (For the purposes of the MCAT, there is little difference between the two hormones, so we cannot eliminate either choice on that basis.)

This question actually tests the concept of negative feedback, the tendency of endocrine glands to overproduce hormones, causing other organs to step in and regulate production. We can glean from the passage that thyroid-stimulating hormone (TSH) produced by the pituitary stimulates the production of T_3 and T_4. On first glance, it might seem that the higher levels of TSH would cause more T_3 production, making I correct. Given the concept of negative feedback, however, we should realize that that elevated TSH is actually a sign that the thyroid is under-producing hormones, causing the pituitary to increase its production of TSH in an effort to regulate the thyroid. Hence, II is actually correct. Because underproduction of thyroid hormones indicates hypothyroidism, III is also correct.

✔ The answer is (C).

3. A 5-year-old has taken 75 mcg of levothyroxine daily for more than a year. The level of free T_4 in his blood has remained at the low end of the reference range. He has begun to report constipation but has shown no signs of excitability or nervousness. Which of the following is likely appropriate?

   A. Dosage of 100 mcg levothyroxine daily.
   B. Dosage of 50 mcg levothyroxine daily.
   C. Daily iodine supplements.
   D. Thalidomide.

This question tested your knowledge of hypothyroidism — that it results in overall lower metabolism, which would include constipation. So it would seem that he is showing symptoms of hypothyroidism. Hence his dosage should be increased. Excitability would be a sign that the child's dosage was already too high, but because that is not the case, (B) is incorrect. Answer choice (C) refers to iodine deficiency as a cause of hypothyroidism, but does not apply here, while answer choice (D) refers to a drug that is actually mentioned as a possible cause of hypothyroidism.

✔ The answer is (A).

4. Which of the following statements about the hypothalamic-pituitary axis is NOT true?

A. It could accurately be described as the coordination of hormone production between the brain and various glands, including the thyroid via the pituitary.

B. It will inhibit the regulation of thyroid hormone via synthetic means by mediating the production of thyroxine.

C. When given signals by the hypothalamus to stimulate TSH production, the pituitary releases T_3 and T_4 hormones.

D. It can trigger hormonal changes in response to external cues such as light and temperature.

We have gleaned from the passage that the process between the hypothalamus, pituitary, and thyroid goes like this: The hypothalamus, as it generally does, monitors various internal and external factors, including light and temperature, making **(D)** true, and triggers the pituitary to release TSH; TSH then triggers the thyroid to release T_3 and T_4 hormones. Because the pituitary does not release T_3 and T_4 hormones, **(C)** is the false statement. Answer choice **(A)** accurately characterizes the process, and answer choice **(B)** is a paraphrase of a statement in the passage: "The delay of hypothalamic-pituitary axis readaptation may postpone the achievement of appropriate TSH levels for several months after the introduction of daily synthetic thyroxine."

✔ The answer is **(C)**.

5. **Diisobutylaluminium hydride (DIBAH) is a reducing agent that is useful in converting esters to aldehydes. Which of the following elements is DIBAH likely to contain in the greatest quantity?**

   A. Oxygen.
   B. Carbon.
   C. Nitrogen.

D. Hydrogen.

To answer this question, you do not need to know anything about DIBAH, but you do need to know what type of reaction it is helping to occur. This type of reaction would be a reduction, which involves the introduction of hydrogen.

✔ Therefore, **(D)** is the correct answer.

6. **A solvent mixture is drawn up a thin sheet of glass coated with silica gel using a capillary tube, resulting in a distribution of analytes on the glass. Which of the following laboratory techniques has been utilized?**

    A. Distillation.
    B. Oxidation.
    C. Chromatography.
    D. Halogenation.

This is a step-by-step description of the process of thin-line chromatography, a separation technique that involves passing a mixture through one of several materials that absorb some of its compounds, causing the various components of the mixture to be distributed in distinct layers. If you did not recognize it right away, you might still have noticed that the process is a type of separation; the only other separation technique among the answer choices was distillation, which involves boiling off substances with lower boiling points to isolate the remaining compounds. The other answer choices represent chemical reactions.

✔ The answer is **(C)**.

bibliography

Association of American Medical Colleges (**www.aamc.org**).

Ferry, Robert J. and Andrew J. Bauer. "Hypothyroidism." EMedicine (**http://emedicine.medscape.com**).

Kaplan. *MCAT Advanced 2009 Edition: Intensive Prep for Top Students.* New York: Kaplan Publishing, 2008.

Orsay, Jonathan. ExamKrackers: *MCAT Complete Study Package,* 7th Edition. New Jersey: Osote Publishing, 2007.

Patterson, Matthew, Jennifer Wooddell, and Jason Faulhaber, M.D. (2008). *The Princeton Review: MCAT Workout: Extra Practice to Help You Ace the Test.* New York: The Princeton Review, Inc, 2007.

Student Doctor Network Forums. "MCAT Discussions." The Student Doctor Network (**http://forums.studentdoctor.net**).

Swift, Jonathan. *A Modest Proposal.* Originally published 1729. Retrieved from Project Gutenberg (**www.gutenberg.org**).

biography

M arti Anne Maguire is a freelance writer and teacher in North Carolina, where she lives with her husband and two children. A former newspaper reporter and high school teacher, she taught her first test prep course more than a decade ago and still teaches test-prep courses in the Raleigh, North Carolina area. She earned her master's degree in journalism from the University of North Carolina at Chapel Hill and her bachelor's degree in English from the University of Florida.

index